This is a progressive club —
All team members now use
the same changing rooms.

FRED TRUEMAN TALKING CRICKET

FRED TRUEMAN
TALKING CRICKET
WITH FRIENDS
PAST AND PRESENT

FRED TRUEMAN WITH DON MOSEY

In association with Scottish Equitable

Hodder & Stoughton

Copyright © 1997 by Fred Trueman and Don Mosey

Illustrations © 1997 by Ed McLachlan

First published in Great Britain in 1997 by
Hodder and Stoughton
a division of Hodder Headline PLC

The right of Fred Trueman and Don Mosey to be identified
as the authors of this work has been asserted by them
in accordance with the Copyright, Designs and
Patents Act 1988.

10 9 8 7 6 5 4 3 2 1

A CIP catalogue record for this title
is available from the British Library

ISBN 0 340 69635 4

Typeset by Hewer Text Composition Services, Edinburgh
Printed and bound in Great Britain
by Mackays of Chatham PLC

Hodder and Stoughton
A division of Hodder Headline PLC
338 Euston Road
London NW1 3BH

Contents

Acknowledgements

The authors gratefully acknowledge the help and support of Scottish Equitable. Our thanks, too, to our Editor, Roddy Bloomfield, for the painstaking care he has exercised in the production of our efforts.

We would also like to thank Ed McLachlan for his brilliant cartoons.

Photographic Acknowledgements

For permission to reproduce copyright photographs, the author and publisher would like to thank The Hulton Deutsch Collection Ltd, The Hulton Getty Collection Ltd, The Keystone Collection, Allsport Photographic Ltd, David Frith.

Foreword

David Henderson, Chief Executive, Scottish Equitable plc

Scottish Equitable is proud to be associated with Fred Trueman in the publication of his new and amusing book of pen-portraits. He has many friends and admirers, in our company and among our clients.

There can be few cricket lovers who have not been entertained on or off the field by Frederick Sewards Trueman, to borrow his own preferred Yorkshire style. Many of us have watched Frederick, or Freddie, or Fred, or FST bowling his heart out in a Test match and there was no finer sight than when he was in full flow. Some of us will remember the day in 1964 when he finally became the first person to take 300 wickets in Test cricket. A smaller number of us are old enough to recall his sensational opening season in Test cricket against India in 1952 when he mesmerized the Indian batsmen who were unaccustomed to bowling of such ferocious pace. He took 29 wickets in that series at just over 13 runs a wicket, including 8 for 31 at Old Trafford. Many more of us have enjoyed his comments on *Test Match Special* spoken in that rich, sonorous and much-imitated voice.

Was Fred Trueman the greatest fast bowler of all? It is the

sort of question which cricket followers like to debate and of course there can be no definitive answer. Few people today are in a position to compare Fred Trueman with, for example, Harold Larwood at his best in the early 1930s, and in any case memories are selective and opinions subjective. One can say, however, that if perhaps not quite the quickest (Frank Tyson might sometimes have been a shade quicker), Fred has been the most successful England fast bowler since the Second World War, and one of the very best from any country. Because of differences in playing conditions and the quality of opponents, statistics cannot tell the full story, but in the absence of other yardsticks they provide a useful guide. Of the more than 30 players who have taken over 200 wickets in Test cricket, only five (the West Indians, Malcolm Marshall, Curtley Ambrose and Joel Garner, and the Pakistanis, Imran Khan and Waqar Younis) have a lower average of runs given away per wicket.

Many Australians might argue that the great Ray Lindwall was a better bowler, and in his playing days Fred himself, never given to false modesty, considered Lindwall his only peer. There were similarities in their bowling styles. Each had a rhythmical and gradually accelerating run-up culminating in an easy and graceful action with a pronounced drag of the right foot, and each bowled mainly late outswingers at great pace. There were also differences – Trueman bowled with a classical side-on action with his arm at its maximum height, while Lindwall was more of a slinger with his arm at times quite low. Both were tremendous cricketers, but let the statistics again have the final word. Trueman took 307 Test wickets at an average of 21.57 runs per wicket and at a strike rate of 4.5 wickets per match, to Lindwall's 228 wickets at an average of 23.03 and a strike rate of 3.7 wickets per match. Each recognized the other's genius and it is a comment on Fred Trueman's eagerness to learn from those he admired that, as readers will discover from these pages, he sought Lindwall's advice on bowling technique.

Fred Trueman would, I believe, despite his love of the traditional forms of cricket, have been a superb performer in today's highly developed one-day game. As a bowler he combined accuracy with hostility, he was a brilliant catcher in close positions who also had a strong throw from the deep, and he was a big-hitting batsman good enough to have scored three centuries in first-class cricket. Indeed with his immense knowledge and understanding of the game, his aggressive approach towards opponents and his desire to win, he would have made an excellent captain in the one-day game. Let us not forget that he captained Yorkshire when they beat the Australians by an innings in 1968.

In *Talking Cricket*, Fred, with his co-author and close friend, Don Mosey, writes about other people, mainly his contemporaries in the game and some of his heroes from earlier generations such as Wilfred Rhodes, Sir Donald Bradman and Harold Larwood, all of whom he came to know well. He also talks about well-known figures from different walks of life such as politics and the stage. Fred's range of friendships is astonishing. His portraits make fascinating reading, particularly with his eye for the funny side and his phenomenal memory. They provide insights about his subjects, but his own character comes through clearly from his observations. Fred is sociable and self-confident, mischievous and rebellious by instinct yet respectful of authority when applied fairly, outspoken and fiercely combative. He loves to talk, often in colourful language, and always with humour. One can also detect in the pages which follow the qualities he admires in his heroes – courage, competitiveness and determination, all good Yorkshire virtues which Fred himself has in abundance. Incidentaly, as readers will learn, he also likes shoes to be clean!

Above all, Fred is an enthusiast and an entertainer. As a player until 1969 he was always fun to watch and since then he has brought pleasure and laughter to millions as broadcaster, after-dinner speaker and raconteur. Fred recognizes, as do we at Scottish Equitable, that cricket is more than just a sport. It is a business which must attract spectators and sponsors and must also encourage young people with sporting talent into the game in competition with other games which may currently offer greater financial rewards. I am happy to commend this vastly entertaining book to all who have an interest in cricket.

Scottish Equitable

Prologue

et's put our cards on the table right from the start. This is
an unashamedly nostalgic and sentimental look at some
of the figures I have known, played with and chatted to during
my time in the game.

Playing for Yorkshire and England were the happiest days
of my life. They brought disappointments as well as successes
but, looking back, I feel an immense satisfaction with the way
cricket changed my life. It gave me friendships which I could
never otherwise have hoped to make; it enabled me to meet
people I could never otherwise have dreamed of encountering;
it allowed me to mingle with some of the greatest legends in
the history of the game.

The purpose of this book is to share those memories – to
introduce the reader to some of those legends and to recall my
conversations with them. I also include, gratefully and happily,
some of the enthusiasts for the game who were perhaps not good
enough to play first-class cricket themselves but who enjoyed it to
the full. Cricket has always been richly blessed with such people.
Many of them were, and are, my good friends; all of them are
people I respect and admire. They are as much a part of my
story as they are a part of my life because cricket is about fun

and laughter as well as about skill and artistry. My memories are of all these things.

This is not to claim that cricket in the years since I retired as a player has not produced its share of personalities, or that there have been no dramatic or spectacular Test series since I hung up my boots. Plainly, those who saw some of the nerve-tingling matches of the 1981 series against Australia will never forget Ian Botham's batting at Headingley and Old Trafford, or his bowling at Edgbaston. The batting of Vivian Richards, Sunil Gavaskar, the Chappell brothers and the Waugh twins, Glenn Turner, Javed Miandad and Asif Iqbal came after my time as a player, as did the bowling of men like Lillee, Roberts, Holding, Garner, Ambrose, Warne, Chandrasekhar, Bedi and Hadlee. I am one of many who regret that political considerations prevented my watching the full flowering of the talent of Barry Richards.

Yet during my thirteen years of Test cricket, greatness was all around me, and it was my privilege to meet, and compete against, most of it. The greatness of former years was in the record books for me to respect and admire. I was privileged to meet and talk to some of the men who established those records in the first place – men like Hirst and Rhodes, Bradman and Headley.

Cricket, I feel, is not the same today as in my day. It is easy to dismiss the great players of the past with the airy solecism: 'Oh, it's a different game from the one you played.' Amongst the better players of my generation there was a general and genuine respect for our contemporaries and those who had gone before us. I don't think this exists today, or at least not to the same extent, and it is a pity. We can all learn from the lessons of history. Consider that Sri Lanka probably won the last World Cup by adhering strictly to the lesson I first learned at the nets as a teenager: bowl line and length; when batting, play straight.

At home I have a painting of Don Bradman batting in his prime. You have only to look at it – head motionless, eyes watchful, balance perfect, bat poised to come down in a

straight line – to recognise genius ... and observation of the basics.

Yes indeed, the game *has* changed, but not necessarily for the better. In the closing pages of this book my friend Peter Parfitt, a man with an excellent cricketing brain, takes a long, intelligent and dispassionate look at the modern game and what he (and I) sees as the causes of its deterioration over the past three or four decades. It should be required reading for the members of the English Cricket Board.

What does concern me is that the money which seems to saturate the game today – from sponsorship, television fees and the very high charges levied for Tests and one-day internationals – is perhaps not being used as wisely as it might.

I was the first to applaud Lord McLaurin's view that younger people were needed on the Cricket Board, yet whose was the first name we saw to be appointed? That of Doug Insole, already aged seventy-one and a 'graduate' of the MCC and TCCB. Is this the sort of progress we can expect?

The counties don't help. Year in year out the same old names, those who have been in power for years, are put forward as representatives to higher authority, however ineffective they have proved to be.

I was never generously rewarded as a player, either for Yorkshire or England, but I make no complaint about that. To play first of all for my county, and then for my country, was simply what youngsters of my day dreamed about. I was therefore horrified to read that modern players are to attend motivation courses. What greater motivation can there be than to pull on an England sweater and go out to compete against the Australians?

I do worry about the attitude of some of our modern players. The pride in representing one's country seems to have been submerged under a blanket of perquisites: huge financial rewards, sponsored cars, mobile phones and all the rest of it. Have they, perhaps, lost sight of what it is all really about?

The players I recall in the following pages enjoyed none of

these rewards. To represent their county or their country always seemed to be reward enough. There was true greatness, but there was also humility and there was respect. The word 'great' seems to be the most overused word in the English language these days – *great* player, *great* shot, *great* delivery – when, to my mind, there is little to establish most of these examples as being out of the ordinary.

I prefer to think that the players I have singled out in this book had something a little bit extra, something rather special which entitled them to be known as *really* great. The non-players, too, were for the most part extraordinary people in themselves. Judge for yourself.

1

Princes and Premiers

Bernard Marmaduke Fitzalan-Howard, Knight of the Garter, Knight Grand Cross of the Royal Victorian Order, Knight Grand Cross of the Order of the British Empire, 16th Duke of Norfolk, Earl of Arundel, Earl of Surrey, Earl Marshal and Hereditary Marshal and Chief Butler of England, was not the sort of chap one would find walking around Scotch Springs, the South Yorkshire village where I was born.

Thirty years later I had moved on a bit, but I was still surprised to find a man whose family titles went back seven or eight centuries managing an England cricket tour to Australia, and I was not the only one. The fact is, however, that His Grace, the Duke of Norfolk was a considerable success as the MCC manager and got on well with the players. As for the Australians . . .

We sailed in the *Canberra* in 1962, and during one of our first meetings the Duke urged the need for a certain delicacy of speech and conduct in the presence of one of our opening batsmen – the Rev. David Sheppard. This advice was not always scrupulously observed, but it's fair to say that when there were breaches of our code of purity, they were accidental or instinctive rather than deliberate.

It was not an entirely smooth voyage to the other side of the world. Ted Dexter was the England captain, and while I have always had the greatest professional respect and personal liking for Ted, there was a general feeling in the game that he had more theories than Darwin and Einstein put together. Thus, when he learned that Gordon Pirie, the distance runner and fitness theorist, was a passenger on board, he decided that here was the perfect way to tune up his players to peak fitness before they landed in Australia.

We were invited to take daily runs round and round the deck of the ship. I forget just how long the circuit was, but it was a pretty long way. We had left England very shortly after the county championship season had ended. During that season I had bowled 1,142 overs for Yorkshire plus another 160 in Tests against Pakistan, and my legs and feet were telling me, loud and clear, that the best way of spending the next few weeks was by having a good rest.

Nevertheless, I tried to show willing by making a token appearance in the first few days of fitness training. I joined the runners, then, at the earliest opportunity, took a short cut across the ship and rejoined the party on the other side.

When Mr Pirie enquired why I was not joining in his exercises with the wholehearted enthusiasm he wanted to see, I told him, very politely, that my thirty-two-year-old legs had had all the toning up they needed during the preceding five months, and if I was going to have to spend the Australian summer bowling at the likes of Bill Lawry, Bobbie Simpson, Norm O'Neill, Neil Harvey, Peter Burge, Brian Booth, Alan Davidson, 'Slasher' Mackay and Richie Benaud – he was at number nine in the batting order! – I felt I knew well enough what they needed.

I had one early run-in with the Duke. He summoned me by barking, 'Trueman,' and pointing to a spot just in front of him.

There was an uneasy silence for a minute before I told His Grace, 'I have a dog at home and I don't talk like that to him,' then turned and walked away.

Some time later he phoned me in my room and said, 'I think you owe me an apology.'

I replied immediately, 'No, sir. I think *you* owe me one.'

I went to see the Duke and we thrashed it out. We shook hands and I never had a wrong word with the manager after that. I like to think that we spent the remainder of the tour as friends, and for long afterwards we exchanged Christmas cards.

It can't have been an easy tour for the Duke. For all his love of cricket and his connection with the higher echelons of the game, he had obviously never spent any length of time in close contact with the game's professionals. Nevertheless, he made every effort to understand any problems we had, and worked very hard to be helpful in whatever way he could, which sometimes rebounded on him. The Duke suffered badly from insomnia, and if he managed a couple of hours' sleep a night he thought he was doing well. He fought his complaint with a steady supply of Grant's Steadfast whisky and extra-strong sleeping pills. He generously told the touring party that if anyone had trouble sleeping, they should contact him. One half of one of his pills should do the trick.

One night in Sydney, His Grace had taken his pills and retired for the night. He was just hovering in that gentle state somewhere between sleep and wakefulness when his telephone rang. Ken Barrington was finding it difficult to get to sleep and could he take up the Duke's kind offer of half a pill? Certainly. Fighting off the sleep which now threatened to overtake him, the manager sat up on the edge of his bed and awaited the arrival of Kenny. Kenny however, had found that the effort of making the phone call had done the trick. He slumped back on his bed, fell fast asleep – and left the Duke waiting all night for his arrival.

In mid-tour there were fears back home for the health of Sir Winston Churchill, and in order to make provisional arrangements for what had to be a state funeral, the Duke of Norfolk flew home. On his return the story went round – and I have never found out how this happened: the Duke was the last person from whom one would have expected indiscretion –

that Churchill had questioned him about certain aspects of the funeral arrangements, asking, in particular, if General de Gaulle would attend. The Duke had told him, 'Of course. That would certainly be expected.'

'In that case,' Sir Winston was said to have insisted, 'make absolutely sure the cortège [carrying his coffin to Blenheim] leaves from Waterloo.'

Sure enough, when the great leader and statesman died in 1965, the coffin was carried from Waterloo Station, no doubt causing considerable problems for British Rail. It has got to be a true story, however it was leaked: the last Churchillian gesture to a Frenchman.

It is one of my great regrets that I never met Sir Winston. I had grown up with an attitude of reverence to the wartime Prime Minister, and when I saw him once, across the road, I was seized by a fierce desire to run over and shake him by the hand.

In contrast to the awe and respect with which we honour our leaders, I was staggered by the Australians' attitude to a man like the Rt Hon. Sir Robert Gordon Menzies, Privy Counsellor, Queen's Counsel, Companion of Honour, Fellow of the Royal Society, and without any doubt the greatest Prime Minister Australia has ever had. When he appeared in the dressing-room during a Test match, the casual greeting from Lindsay Hassett and company was something like: 'Hi, Bob. How're you? Good on yer.'

It took me some time to realise that this was most certainly not a case of familiarity having bred contempt. The Aussies thought just as much of their Prime Minister as we did of ours. They just, as ever, expressed it in a different way. Like all great men, Menzies had the common touch – *par excellence*. He absolutely loved his cricket. He once told me Ray Lindwall and I could have been related because we had the same near-perfect action. Aussies liked me, he said, 'because I would have a go'. It's a complex term, but I knew what he meant.

I believe it was Bob who initiated the one-day match between touring sides and the Prime Minister's XI which took place in Canberra. I played in one of these and, to my utter delight, found Bob had persuaded Don Bradman to come out of retirement and take part. The ground was completely packed, and when The Don came out to bat there was something like pandemonium. Everyone stood; everyone applauded; everyone cheered. People were knocked down by the press of photographers fighting to get a picture of the scene.

I thought, now, perhaps, I will get one last chance to bowl at the greatest of all batsmen, but it was not to be. Brian Statham was in action: Bradman played a ball defensively, it rolled back, hit the stumps and dislodged a bail. I looked round waiting for the umpire to have a moment of inspiration and shout 'No ball', but there was no such moment. My last chance had come and gone.

There was still something left in the day for me, however. It was 6 February, and at dinner that evening, the Prime Minister of Australia stood and said, 'Today is a very special day for me – and for one of my guests. It is Freddie Trueman's birthday and I have a little present for him,' and he handed me a tankard inscribed: 'Happy birthday – R. Menzies.' It is one of my proudest possessions.

The first British Prime Minister I met was Sir Anthony Eden, the 1st Earl of Avon. As a very small boy visiting the cinema, I had seen him on newsreels as a handsome Foreign Secretary – I believe he was a bit of a heart-throb with the ladies back then – and it never occurred to me that I would one day meet him. During the tour to the West Indies in 1959–60 we had played in a high-scoring draw in Barbados and gone on to meet the Leeward Islands in Antigua, where Brian Statham and I were taking a rest. I was astonished when Sir Anthony appeared, and even more so when he sat down to talk to the two of us. He asked if we would like to have lunch with him the following day, fixed things up with the manager and sent an official-looking limousine to pick us up.

Sir Anthony was living in a splendid ranch-type villa with a swimming-pool fed by the sea, and it was the perfect place to relax. We had coffee, a swim, lunch and another swim and, not for the first time, I was intrigued by how many politicians have a love of cricket. Sir Anthony talked a lot about Len Hutton and told us how, in 1956, he had sought the views of Commonwealth countries and received favourable answers, before awarding Len his knighthood. I felt I had been let into some kind of state secret and wrote home rather excitedly to tell my mum and dad.

Sir Anthony also told us how he had never realised the immense interest in cricket – and particularly Test cricket – amongst Commonwealth leaders. When, one March, he sent out invitations to a Commonwealth conference in London, most of the acceptances he received asked for a date in June so they could attend the Lord's Test match.

I met Harold Macmillan (later the Earl of Stockton) during a Test at The Oval. He joined the players for lunch and, lingering a little while afterwards, noticed me still in the dining room with my coffee and pipe. He joined me and asked if I often sat on my own like that. I told him that while I enjoyed the company of my team-mates as much as the next man, there were times when I preferred to sit quietly by myself and have a good think. We then talked cricket for a long time and I found him a most interesting and sympathetic man.

Sir Harold Wilson was a man I regarded as a great friend, despite the fact that we were very much on opposite sides of the political fence. Perhaps it was that as a couple of Yorkshiremen we understood each other. Once, at a dinner at which we were both guests, I passed my tobacco-pouch down the table to him when the speeches began. It came back with a note: 'Thank you for the tobacco. Being a true Yorkshireman I filled *both* my pipes.' I've still got that note somewhere.

It was Harold Wilson who once described me as 'the greatest living Yorkshireman'. He told me afterwards that he received only one critical comment on this – from the writer J. B. Priestley.

We had many fascinating conversations but none more so than the one when Don Mosey and I were writing a book called *Fred Trueman's Yorkshire*. The two of us were broadcasting on a Lord's Test match at the time, so we arranged to be a bit late on parade one morning and made an appointment to see Sir Harold. We met him in his private office at Westminster. My word, we covered a lot of ground – his boyhood, days at Oxford (as student and don), his first ministerial appointments, his support of Huddersfield Town FC, the British film industry . . . It was a truly memorable couple of hours.

In August 1964 when I took my 300th Test wicket, Sir Harold rang me up at home and told me, 'This will be recognised.' I am absolutely certain he recommended a knighthood for me, and I am equally certain that someone at Lord's put the block on it.

Baroness Thatcher (at that time simply Mrs Margaret Thatcher) was a lady I admired tremendously. It was at her invitation that Veronica and I visited 10 Downing Street, although her interest in cricket was minimal. Nevertheless, I was delighted to meet her and it was no great effort to chat with her about other things.

I knew John Major before and after he became Prime Minister and always found him a delightful man. He would have loved to play cricket, but a motorcycle accident as a young man ruled that out. Still, he has compensated by his enthusiastic support for the game and never misses an opportunity to have an hour or two at a Test match.

We once found ourselves in different boxes at Lord's and exchanged greetings by a wave of the hands. Shortly afterwards there was a knock at the door of the box I was in, and there was the Prime Minister asking if he might come in to have a word with me! He stayed for some time, then took the trouble to write from 10 Downing Street to my host, expressing his thanks for the hospitality he had received.

I have seen John Major at a private ground in Oxfordshire with his jacket off bowling to a couple of youngsters. He is utterly without pretensions and a very much stronger character than some newspapers would have us believe. I think of him as a thoroughly nice, honest, straightforward man.

John Paul Getty, third son of an American financial wizard, lives in London and has proved a wonderful benefactor to many organisations, not least to the game of cricket. I would not dream of going to Lord's without visiting Mr Getty in his box. He was also a great friend of Brian Johnston, with whom he shared – and I always find this a bit difficult to credit – a love of the Australian soap opera *Neighbours*. To hear the two of them swopping reactions to various twists and turns in the ongoing plots made you wonder if you were in the same world as the one you woke up in that morning!

Sir William Worsley, President of Yorkshire County Cricket Club from 1961 to 1973, was one of my favourite people and a very great friend to me, and I enjoyed playing on that lovely private ground of his at Hovingham Hall. The team were entertained to dinner at the hall after winning the championship in 1959, which is the only time I can remember anything being celebrated by the county club – at least as far as the players were concerned – during my time. It must underline the sense of relief felt in Yorkshire that another championship had at last been won. (If they ever do it again, I can't think *how* they will celebrate.)

I remember Sir William walking out to greet me as I came off the field during a match at Headingley, offering his congratulations on my taking my 1,000th wicket. *I* didn't know that had happened, but *he* did – don't ask me how – and it's a fair indication of how Sir William valued the club's history and traditions.

Sir William was one of those who urged me to concentrate more on my batting, like Maurice Leyland and Herbert Sutcliffe. In a way, this attention was flattering, but impractical. How was I expected to bowl fast for a major part of the opposition's innings, field in a close-catching position requiring maximum concentration . . . and bat as well?

Nevertheless, Sir William was quite insistent that I could score well if I put my mind to it, and when, in 1963, I got 104 against Northants he sent me a note – 'Now you have done it, do it again' – and enclosed a cheque for ten pounds. I couldn't resist a little smile. Keith Andrew (of all people) had dropped me behind the stumps off Colin Milburn when I was in the seventies.

Lieutenant-Colonel Doctor Fatehsinghrao Gaekwad succeeded his father as Maharajah of Baroda in 1951. When the Indian Government abolished princely titles in 1970, he continued to play a part in the political, industrial and sporting development of his country. He was my friend for many years and I knew him simply as 'Jackie' Baroda, not so much with familiarity as affection and respect because he was a great gentleman – one of the finest I have ever known.

I first met Jackie in 1952 when he enthusiastically supported the Indian touring team in England. Seven years later he managed the tourists. It was after I had retired, however, that we became much better acquainted. He was a close friend of two other pals of mine, Claude and Morag Brownlow, and used often to stay at their home in Tiptree, Essex, when he was in England. Together with Don Mosey and our wives, we all stayed with the Brownlows on the weekend of Test matches at Lord's and The Oval, and these visits used to follow a set pattern. On Sunday mornings, Claude, Don and I were joined by one of Claude's business partners for a round of golf at Colchester. We would leave Jackie with the ladies gathered around him beside the Brownlows' swimming-pool, in the manner, we thought, of his palace handmaidens back in Baroda. While we were golfing, Jackie would tell the ladies of his upbringing in India, when he had indulged in such requirements of a princeling's education as hunting tigers on elephant-back. This had obviously left its mark on him in some way because, as an adult, Jackie became an enthusiastic conservationist and a trustee of the World Wildlife Fund.

A little man with dark, twinkling eyes, a neat beard and a considerable appetite for Glen Morangie malt whisky, Jackie was a most entertaining companion and raconteur.

For many years he kept a flat in London as a base for visits. The first of these was in Chelsea, and his next-door neighbour was the tenor, Placido Domingo. It rather tickled Jackie that when Domingo was rehearsing, he would get a free concert!

Jackie loved parties and regularly threw his own, notably during the Lord's Test match during the time when he had a flat in Maida Vale. Afterwards he would take Veronica and myself, Claude and Morag, Don and his wife Jo, to a Chinese restaurant on the Edgware Road where the proprietors knew and loved him. Jackie took a party of us there to celebrate the birthdays of Veronica and the Brownlows' daughter Catriona, on the eighth day of the eighth month of 1988. The superstitious Chinese gave us champagne on the house when the birth of a daughter to the Duke and Duchess of York was announced that day.

It was from that same restaurant that I once put Jackie into a London taxi and asked the driver to take 'His Highness' home. It was an evening when Jackie had been enjoying the Glen Morangie, and the egalitarian-minded cabbie, after a quick glance at his passenger, told me, 'I don't care about the title, guv, so long as 'is 'ighness 'as got the fare.' I had to assure him that he would be paid.

I ran into Jackie one night in Bangkok airport as I waited for the overnight flight to Heathrow. He was fast asleep, so I dropped into the next chair and started reading a newspaper. He woke, glanced at his companion and shouted, 'Freddie!' and we had a most pleasant reunion. Having established that we were due to travel on the same plane, he disappeared for a minute to 'fix things', and we were given adjoining first-class seats. I remember that we talked cricket all night, rather to the annoyance of a passenger in front of us who was trying to sleep.

For a worldly man who had travelled extensively, Jackie had an almost childlike innocence in other contexts. One Sunday evening, Veronica and I, Jo and Don, were leaving the Brownlows' home to go to our hotel in London. Claude and Morag, together with Jackie, their house guest, took us to the station at Kelvedon. A train approached at high speed and Jackie stepped forward with an arm raised in a signal for it to stop. It might have worked on the Baroda state line, but the driver of the British Rail nonstop Norwich to Liverpool Street express wasn't impressed. As the train hurtled through at eighty miles an hour we had to grab the maharajah and haul him to safety.

As President of the Board of Control for cricket in India, Jackie did an enormous amount of work to bring about the resumption of Tests between India and Pakistan. He also travelled the globe on World Wildlife Fund business, and kept his friends in touch through an annual newsletter which usually read like an account of Marco Polo's adventures. He was a dear and valued friend and we were deeply sorry when he died.

2

Cricket and the Arts

For as long as I can remember there has been a close, and always cordial, link between cricket and the arts – in particular, the stage. You only have to look at the history, and the membership, of the Lord's Taverners to realise how strong this bond is, although it goes back a lot further than that.

Perhaps the earliest direct link was established by the man who later became Sir Charles Aubrey Smith, the grand old man of Hollywood, where he died in 1948. It was as plain Mr Smith that he captained Sussex in 1877 and 1888, after winning four Blues at Cambridge. On 12 and 13 March 1889, he had the unique distinction of skippering England in the only Test he ever played, against South Africa in Port Elizabeth. Smith was leading a side raised by Major Robert Gardner Warton and the match was the seventeenth of the tour. It was only later that the game was elevated to Test match status and thus became the first Test meeting of England and South Africa.

How I would have loved to meet this magnificent figure of a fine old English gentleman – well over six feet tall with a grand sweep of a moustache – but he was well before my time, of course. I did, however, see him in wonderful films like *The Lives of a Bengal Lancer*, *The Prisoner of Zenda* and

The Four Feathers, even though I had no idea, at the time, that this imposing figure had actually played cricket at all, let alone first-class and then Test cricket. What I can say is that I have played at the Sir Charles Aubrey Smith Bowl in Hollywood, where I met his widow. She must have been well into her nineties when I visited the film capital with Yorkshire CCC, on a private tour in 1964–5, and was an enthusiastic supporter of the Hollywood club which had given her husband so much pleasure.

We met most of Hollywood's cricket enthusiasts on that trip, and for our part we were tickled pink at being closely involved with some very famous names in the world of entertainment. During a party round a swimming-pool one evening, we were out to impress a couple of the local belles – Jackie Collins, successful writer of popular fiction, and Mamie Van Doren, a blonde starlet whose impressive pneumatic charms had graced one or two B-movies. Foremost amongst those trying to make a favourable impression was our intrepid captain, D. B. Close.

For most of his life, Closey has had a wide range of party tricks, most of which have displayed his strength and dexterity. In Hollywood he must have decided that something new was called for, because he started diving over a chair into the pool. Then it was two chairs, then three. Finally, a table was put in place as well as the chairs and Closey tried to launch himself over the top of the entire range of furniture, into the pool. Of course, it had to happen: the whole issue was crushed into matchwood as the captain's bulk – which was considerable – hit chairs and table, and man and splinters shunted into the pool. I think he did, finally, manage to catch the attention of the ladies but perhaps not in the way he had intended.

Parties and swimming-pools seem to go together and, at least in my experience, someone is always fated to end up in the pool, affording much more amusement to the onlookers than the victim. It happened to me in Sydney. The party was given by John (later Sir John) Mills, along with his wife and their younger daughter, Hayley, who would be six or seven years old at the time. The guests included two of the stars of a film John had been making out there, *The Summer of the Seventeenth Doll*, who were to become two of the biggest names in Hollywood – Anne Baxter and Ernest Borgnine.

John had asked along the MCC touring party, and in the middle of all the fun and games I found myself hurled, fully clothed, into the pool. I had no idea who had done it, having had only a brief glimpse of a white shirt as I was dumped into the water, but I had my suspicions. As I sat, dripping wet and feeling distinctly disgruntled, the suspicions grew into certainty that my assailant had been an Australian actor who was one of the revellers. I waited my moment, then pounced, and dumped him into the middle of the pool. It was some time before the others could convince me I had picked on the wrong man! It was even longer – years, in fact – before I learned who was the real culprit: my team-mate and long-time friend, Trevor Bailey. I have a long memory . . .

It must have been all of ten years later that Trevor and I

found ourselves on opposing sides, in a county championship game at Leyton. Trevor came in to bat and was startled when I let a bouncer go which whistled past his ears. A bouncer . . . in the matey atmosphere of a festival . . . from an old pal? Trevor gave me a long, long look which plainly asked, 'What was all that about?'

I gave him a straight answer: 'That's for shoving me in the swimming-pool in Sydney.'

Trevor gazed at me down the pitch, wide eyed and open mouthed, for a minute, then gasped, 'You've remembered that for all these years?'

'I have,' I retorted, and he threw his head back and roared with laughter, in which I promptly joined. Around ten thousand spectators must have wondered what on earth was happening out in the middle.

That party in Sydney followed an afternoon's play between the MCC and New South Wales, a game in which I was playing and my new-ball colleagues, Brian Statham and Peter Loader, were not. With the MCC batting during the afternoon, I was sitting in the dressing-room when I was called to the phone. It was the NSW secretary, who told me, 'There's a man down here asking for you. He says he is John Mills, the actor.' I went downstairs and, sure enough, it was John. I fixed up a ticket for him and took him up to the dressing-room.

John hadn't been there long before I was called to the phone once again. This time the secretary said, 'There's another actor here asking for you. He's called Trevor Howard.'

Down I went again and, indeed, found Trevor there. He had finished filming a new version of *Mutiny on the Bounty*, in which he played the old Charles Laughton role of Captain Bligh – a film which, incidentally, Trevor loved. Trevor Howard was a keen student of the game of cricket. I believe he had it written into contracts that he was always free for the period of the Lord's Test, and he would fly back from wherever he was filming to attend the game as a member of the MCC. So keen was he, in fact, that I have known him arrange publicity tours for his films to countries where England were playing a Test series, so he could take time off from his duties to attend the games. So we now had two well-known English actors sitting in the MCC dressing-room drinking beer. You'll know how things are said to go in threes, so when the phone rang for the third time I didn't have to ask whether the call was for me.

The new arrival was my good friend Terry-Thomas. Finding himself at a loose end after completing his part in the film *It's a Mad, Mad, Mad, Mad World* in Hollywood, he had remembered that the MCC were playing in Australia, and booked himself a flight across the Pacific 'to watch a bit of cricket'. So he joined the party which was now beginning to warm up in our dressing-room.

We had to go out to field for the last session of the day, so with supplies of beer in the dressing-room fridge running a bit low, Statham and Loader took our three guests on a tour of the bars in the Sydney Cricket Ground, and there are quite a few of them. As I went out to field I remember musing idly that that must have been as accomplished a quintet of English drinkers as ever assembled on an Australian cricket ground: Statham, Loader, Mills, Howard and Terry-Thomas . . . what a bunch! I reckoned that Sydney must be wondering what had hit it.

It was, I reflected later, another example of how cricket, and the performing arts, have enjoyed a long and affectionate association. Many actors have loved to spend their time watching cricket, which is how the Lord's Taverners came into existence in the first place; and many cricketers have found pleasure in the theatre. To this day, I prefer watching a theatrical performance to films or television, and my personal friendships with actors and variety-entertainers have given me immense pleasure and a fund of precious memories.

Terry-Thomas, for instance – how much fun I had with him! We enjoyed our parties, it's true, but always with an awareness that we had a job to do as well. I recall one tremendous party while I was taking part in a Test at Lord's and T-T was appearing at the Palladium. T-T had a Jensen sports car at the time, and as we drove back to his flat he insisted that I stayed the night.

The following morning I was awakened by that silky voice announcing, 'Good morning, sir. Your tea is served.' And there he was in the doorway, immaculately dressed in a schoolboy uniform of cap, blazer, flannels and tie, bearing a tray with a teapot, cup and saucer, sugar and milk. We went off to Lord's, where I took a few wickets against New Zealand and held three catches. T-T occupied his usual spot under the committee room at Lord's and enjoyed a convivial day.

When I next encountered him he congratulated me on England's victory, and I enquired how his evening's performance had gone at the Palladium.

'Absolutely splendidly,' he smiled. 'In fact I think it was one of the finest performances I have ever given: I over-ran by at least ten minutes. I gave them the one about the farmer who was troubled because his tup was not performing very well, so he consulted the vet who gave him some tablets, urging him not to give the ram more than one at a time. At the next consultation, the vet was delighted to learn that the tup was now performing quite satisfactorily after one tablet, and enquired what the farmer had done with the remaining supply. The farmer didn't give him a direct answer but said the tablets had tasted very strongly of peppermint. And the audience loved it, old man . . . absolutely loved it. Yes, indeed. I think it was quite one of my finest performances.'

I once met Errol Flynn, on my way back from a West Indian tour, and was surprised to find what a well-built specimen he was. I know he played heroic roles in Hollywood, but in films all kinds of tricks can be worked. Alan Ladd, for instance, wasn't exactly Mr Universe, and I don't think Mel Gibson, of more recent vintage, is. Flynn, however, was the genuine article, and what a life he led. As an Australian from Tasmania, he knew his cricket, so we got along very well. Michael Wilding was another, very English, actor I came to know well, and I also met Anna Neagle, so often Michael's leading lady.

One of the nicest people I *ever* met – one who became a very close friend and whose death saddened me enormously – was Leslie Crowther. I first encountered him in Scarborough, where he was appearing in the Fol-de-Rols, and from there he went on to a brilliant career on stage and television. He was an incredible ad-libber, could adopt any accent known to man or beast, and was one of the most accomplished after-dinner speakers I have ever heard. However, it was as a genuine, warm-hearted human being that I remember Leslie most of all, together with his lovely wife, Jean, and their family.

The Black and White Minstrels could almost have been signed up as an integral part of Yorkshire County Cricket Club, so close did our association become. That also started in Scarborough and continued as long as the Black and Whites remained together. Three of the Yorkshire players – Philip Sharpe, Don Wilson and Tony Nicholson – knew the Black and Whites' routines so well that they could entertain the rest of us for hours by going through them. The musical quality might not have been quite the same, but they were word-perfect. Principals like Tony Mercer, Dai Francis and John Boulter were as familiar in our dressing-room as we were in theirs, but the whole company were great friends with all our players and it was a very happy association indeed.

That brings me to Harry Secombe – Sir Harry. What an utterly delightful man! On the evening after I had taken my 300th Test wicket at The Oval he had me up on stage at the theatre where he was playing as Mr Pickwick, and presented me with a tape-recorder, so that for ever afterwards I would be able to listen to the radio commentary on that moment.

Harry was a man who loved his cricket as much as he loved to laugh and make others laugh, and he was no mean performer with the bat, either. Keith Miller recalls once playing against Harry in a charity match and playfully bowling him a bouncer.

Harry didn't turn a hair: he swung round and hooked the ball for four!

Harry, with Dame Vera Lynn, was associated with a charity which organised a cricket match at Bromley Park in Kent as one of the regular fund-raising efforts. I played in a number of matches there and it was wonderful to see the turn-out of stars for the Showbiz XI: David Tomlinson, Ian Carmichael, Charlie Drake, Eric Sykes, Pete Murray ... which reminds me of the time Pete came in to bat and Harry Secombe said to me, 'Go off your full run and bowl him a bouncer. Make sure it's outside the off-stump, of course. We don't want anybody hurt.'

So, I marked out the full run and Pete Murray looked up in surprise: 'What's going on?' In I came and bowled a fairly quick one, but, as instructed, well wide of the off-stump and past the batsman. It was then that we found that somebody had been hurt, after all. It wasn't the batsman, but the wicket-keeper. Everyone had been told to move a bit deeper to keep up the charade, and the slips had gone back, but the wicket-keeper was Eric Sykes – and we had forgotten that Eric was a bit deaf. He was still standing about five or six yards back and as he took the ball he damaged a finger. It wasn't broken but it was a bit bent. Eric was involved at the time in filming a comedy in which he played the part of a Mexican bandit or something of the kind. Filming had to be delayed for several weeks because the role called for him to strum a guitar ... and he couldn't!

Tommy Trinder was another from the world of showbiz who became a great friend. Once, during a flight from Edinburgh to London, he told me about the time he was recovering from a patch of ill-health so went to Australia to enjoy a bit of sunshine. As soon as he got there he was asked to do some work, and ended up doing as much entertaining as he would have done if he had stayed at home. 'But,' he added with a grin, 'I earned enough to buy myself a block of flats in Sydney.'

Paul Carpenter, the Canadian actor, used to spend a lot of time in our dressing-room when I was playing in London, and I spent hours yarning with him. The story I like best which involved Paul, actually comes from my associate Don Mosey.

One of Don's great friends at the BBC was John Fenton, the golf broadcaster, who, in his younger days, was a BBC engineer. John was sound-effects man on a radio programme called *Riders of the Range*, which used to be transmitted on Sunday evenings in the days when almost all programmes were live and sound-effects were produced naturally, and not pre-recorded, as they are nowadays. *Riders of the Range* was, of course, a pseudo-western series starring Paul Carpenter. Another prominent member of the cast was Rustler the dog. Rustler was a huge, ferocious-looking Alsatian, trained to respond to signals – if the script called for a bark, Rustler would provide it. Unfortunately, he had been trained, at an earlier stage of his career, to react (violently) to the sound of a pistol shot. While *Riders of the Range* was far from being a *violent* programme – violence on a BBC radio programme in the 1940s on a Sunday evening? Of course not – one week the script, by Charles Chilton, called for a shot to be fired.

Unknown to anyone else, the young sound-effects engineer, John Fenton, had an absolute and abject fear of dogs in general, and Rustler the Alsatian in particular. Nevertheless, during the series he had overcome this fear to a certain extent, and, in any case, Rustler was safely tethered to the leg of a very large concert grand piano, which was a normal part of the furnishings of the Piccadilly Studios, where *Riders of the Range* was staged before an audience.

The fateful evening arrived. Fenton checked out his props – coconut shells for the sound of horses' hooves, and the rest of his paraphernalia – and, right on cue, fired his pistol shot. It was at that moment that Rustler (who had no part in that scene and was enjoying a quiet sleep against the piano leg) came rapidly back to life. He was, as I have said, a very *large* dog. He now started across the stage in the direction of the man who had fired a pistol, towing the concert grand piano in his wake! As the growling, slavering monster approached, the

young sound-effects engineer fled the scene – and the theatre –
leaving Paul Carpenter, the musical group Sons of the Saddle,
and the rest of the cast, falling about with laughter. And all in
front of a live audience!

Let me be the first to concede that there has been a fair bit
of name-dropping so far, but I'm not the first one to indulge in
that. Brian Johnston used to describe E. W. ('Jim') Swanton,
cricket correspondent emeritus of the *Daily Telegraph*, as 'such
a snob he wouldn't ride in the same car as his chauffeur'.
That was, in fact, a paraphrase of an earlier epigram by Ian
Peebles, the Middlesex cricketer, journalist and wit, but Brian
used to trot it out with great glee, and it was a fact that Jim
Swanton had a considerable fondness for celebrities, especially
those with titles.

Thus it was that in company with Peter Richardson, Don
Wilson, Peter Parfitt and others I went to a ground in Kent
to play in a game to mark the opening of a new pavilion, or
something of the sort, and before the start I was startled to see
E. W. Swanton arrive.

'Hey,' I said to Richardson, 'look who's come: EWS, and
we haven't anybody here from the nobility for him to frater-
nise with.'

I should mention for the benefit of anyone who doesn't
already know it, that throughout his playing days 'Pakistan
Pete' seemed to regard it as his major mission in life to take
a rise out of Swanton. He went to enormous lengths to do this
and was largely successful. Richardson was also undoubtedly
the best-known practical joker on the first-class circuit. When
I mentioned our possible dilemma at the match in Kent, he
therefore replied, 'No problem.'

Playing in the match was a young actor, a member of a
repertory company, to whom Richardson then said, 'You,
my friend, today are the third son of the Earl of Carlisle.
Just remember that whoever speaks to you and no matter what about ... the third son of the Earl of Carlisle
...' With that, he quietly circulated the news through the

assembled throng that we had a member of a titled family in our midst.

It didn't take long for the intelligence to reach the distinguished journalist. Like a shot he moved in to sit beside the young man at lunch and when the 'earl's son' took a wicket or two bowling indifferent slow left-arm, Jim was heard to mumble that 'he showed considerable promise'.

Yes, I don't think Jim Swanton would be a keen advocate of the abolition of the House of Lords and he certainly wouldn't favour the abolition of hereditary peers.

3

===

On the Box

One way and another, I suppose I've had my fair share of involvement in television during the past forty years or so, but I can't think of anything which has given me more pleasure than the week I spent filming with the cast of *Dad's Army*.

I've completely forgotten the name of the place – somewhere in Norfolk masquerading as 'Warmington-on-Sea' – but I certainly haven't forgotten any of the characters in that wonderful series. Some became firm friends and the friendships have endured; some, sadly, are no longer with us, but I remember them all with affection and with gratitude for the way they welcomed me and made me feel perfectly at home. What a wonderful bunch of actors they were and what an absolutely splendid bunch of blokes!

There were no stars, no principal players or supporting cast. They were simply a bunch of friends, enjoying an experience together, much as Brian Johnston used to describe the *Test Match Special* commentary operation. Most of all, they were a *team*, and they worked exactly like some of the sporting teams with which I had been involved. Every character had a chance to be the star of the show at one moment or another, perhaps merely by a facial expression or the flickering of an eye, but every expression, every word, every movement, was an essential part of the whole show. It was an education to me to see them at work, I can tell you.

The story of that particular episode was, briefly, that Bill Pertwee's team of air-raid wardens played a cricket match against Arthur Lowe's team of Home Guards and, true to form, the despicable warden Hodges had roped in a secret weapon to play for his side: F. S. Trueman. I had to bowl at Captain Mainwaring from a run which took me out of the ground completely, and jump over a wall on my subsequent approach to the wicket.

That's about all I *can* remember of the plot, but what I do remember, with great clarity, was the enormous fun we had during that week of filming. All the cast, to a greater or lesser extent, were cricket followers and they were all delighted to talk to me about cricket at some stage during that week. In fact they wanted to talk cricket when I would have been happier to ask about some of *their* experiences.

I was startled one day when that lovely man Arnold Ridley – as quiet and gentle as his character of Private Godfrey, the medical orderly with the weak bladder – took me to one side and shyly told me how his father had taken him, as a small boy, to Bristol and introduced him to W. G. Grace! This really rocked me, I can tell you.

I had talked to Wilfred Rhodes who had *bowled* at Grace, and to Rhodes he was merely an opponent – a formidable and famous one, it's true, but just another player, nevertheless. Now here was a man who *wasn't* a cricketer and who regarded Grace with the awe and respect due to the greatest name of nineteenth century cricket, telling me how the Doctor bent over and gravely shook his hand and signed his autograph album. It somehow put it all into proper perspective. We were filming a television programme in the second half of the twentieth century, and here was one of the actors talking to me about meeting the most impressive figure of the previous century, the man who established most of the earliest records in the game.

It was a truly magic moment in my life. And do you know what Arnold remembered most clearly of the meeting? How surprised he was that such a huge figure of a man, with a massive growth of beard, had such a high-pitched, squeaky voice!

My personal friendship with Bill Pertwee continued long after that, and I was delighted to see him at my sixty-fifth birthday celebration in London in February 1997. He is (I need hardly say) an entirely different person from the character he played in *Dad's Army*. Some years after I had played for his cricket team he invited Veronica and me to a film show at the Imperial War Museum, and he chose to screen the episode of *Dad's Army* in which I had appeared. It was only then that I learned of the existence of the Dad's Army Association (I refuse to call it a fan club), and that its secretary comes from just a few miles from my home in Yorkshire.

Dad's Army went on a stage-tour of the country, and while it was playing at the Alhambra Theatre in Bradford, Bill Pertwee and John Le Mesurier (Sergeant Wilson) came out to my home for lunch and we had a good old natter about my week with the company. They also helped me answer a letter I had received from a gentleman who had written to ask for my help with his bowling. He had (he said) suddenly developed a fault which resulted in the ball leaving his hand, failing to bounce, and it was still rising as it passed over the wicket-keeper's head! What bewildered him most was that the fault had only recently developed, after he had passed his forty-ninth birthday. I am not sure our reply was entirely helpful, but at least we did our best.

On a later occasion, Veronica and I had a visit from another member of the cast of *Dad's Army* – Ian Lavender (Private Pike, that 'stupid boy'), who was also playing in Bradford but in a different show. He arrived with yet another old pal, Bill Maynard (later to become Claude Jeremiah Greengrass in *Heartbeat*). Ian rushed to a window and started to identify the topographical features which could be seen from there. I was astonished at this, but it turned out that Ian had attended prep school at

Flasby Hall, a former stately home which is screened by trees at the bottom of my garden.

I had met Bill Maynard some years previously, when he was playing in Scarborough. We were both going to play in a benefit match at Helmsley, some miles inland, and Bill picked me up at home (at that time in Scarborough) in an open-topped Ford Zephyr. Cigarette packets, sweet-wrappings and assorted rubbish had collected over what must have been several years in the back of the car. I christened it there and then (and still think of it now) as 'the flying dustbin'. It was during that game at Helmsley that I witnessed one of the most remarkable shots I have ever seen on a cricket field. Someone bowled Bill a full toss, and with a cross-bat swipe, he smashed the ball, straight as an arrow and only a few feet high, back past the bowler and out of the ground.

To my great regret, I never actually appeared in *All Creatures Great and Small*, that delightful series set in the North Yorkshire Dales and based on the books of Alf Wight, the veterinary surgeon of Thirsk who was perhaps better known as James Herriot. I did, however, once receive what you might call a 'mention'. The producer telephoned and asked permission to use my name in one episode and I gladly concurred. The context, as you might expect, was a cricket match in which I was supposed to be playing.

So Freddie Trueman duly appeared in the match at 'Darrowby', but he was played by a young actor. I was never told why this was, although I would gladly have appeared, as I had done in *Dad's Army*, I watched the episode and I have to say that the actor didn't look much like me, either in appearance or performance, but probably that wasn't too important. The story, like all Herriot's, was as pleasant and wholesome as ever.

I was, however, very glad to meet Alf Wight, a modest, unassuming man, who used to lunch regularly at a pub near Ripon which was run by a friend of Veronica's and mine. Don Mosey was there, too, and from that meeting there is one little gem we both remember vividly.

The chat was tape-recorded to use in a book, and when we transcribed the recording, one of Alf's comments came out like this: responding to a question about Yorkshire farmers' reactions to being visited by the local vet who happened to be a successful author he said, 'When a chap's got a sick cow worth four hundred pounds he doesn't want Charles Dickens walking in to attend to it.' We sent the transcription of the whole recording off to Alf for his approval and it came back with just one thing altered – £400 for the value of the cow had been changed to £600. I remember Don remarking to me that cattle prices went up rather quickly at Thirsk Auction Mart!

Alf was a gentle and kindly man who always seemed just a bit overwhelmed by the fame which had overtaken him when he set down a few of his real-life experiences as a Dales vet. Although Sunderland-born and brought up in Glasgow, he developed a great love for Yorkshire in general and the Dales in particular. As 'James Herriot' he was immensely successful in the United States. He often found his veterinary clinic filled with American visitors wanting books autographed, although he was always at great pains to keep his professional and literary lives quite separate and distinct. I was very fond of the man.

One of my earliest ventures in television was in a Yorkshire programme called *Sometimes You Win* in which three of us had to forecast likely draws for the benefit of football pools punters. Of course, nowhere was it more likely to attract the attention of a know-it-all than in my native county! A bloke in Bradford wrote to say he could do better than the three of us put together, so he was invited to take part. As we all expected, he made a complete dog's breakfast of his appearance, but, far worse as things turned out, he had taken a day off work to appear, without his boss's approval, and he got sacked.

I presented *The Indoor League* – of competitive games which didn't require a field or stadium – which ran for three or four years on Yorkshire TV. In Cardiff I was very proud to take part in a radio programme with Simon Weston, the dreadfully injured and disfigured hero of the Falklands War. I also appeared on

The Dickie Henderson Show and *What's My Line?*, and I have become something of a season ticket-holder on *This is Your Life*. Apart from being the subject of that programme, I have lost count of the number of other people's shows on which I have made an appearance.

Back in Yorkshire, I interviewed Charlie Williams on what was, I believe, his first TV appearance. It was always said that the first black or Asian comedian to achieve success on television would make a million. Well, Charlie was coloured, and a Doncaster Rovers footballer into the bargain when he appeared on TV for the first time. I don't know whether he has achieved millionaire's status yet, but I do know he is a thoroughly nice chap and a damn good comedian, too. For several years I have run a golf tournament for charity, the Freddie Trueman Classic, in Harrogate; Charlie was always one of my guest celebrities and never let me down.

I was once flown out to Jamaica with the actor William Franklyn to make one of his celebrated Schweppes advertisements, and in the USA I made another advertisement for Miller beer. Then there was the Terry Wogan chat show, and I suppose I may have forgotten one or two along the way.

For sheer, sustained pleasure over a whole week, nothing has equalled the fun and pleasure of making that one *Dad's Army* episode, however, and every time I see one of the repeats on TV I remember it with great affection. Some years after it was recorded, Bill Pertwee joined us in the *Test Match Special* box at Headingley one weekend for the feature called 'A View from the Boundary', in which Brian Johnston interviewed, during the Saturday luncheon-break, a well-known personality who was a cricket enthusiast but not a cricket *player*. They were marvellous pieces of radio broadcasting because Brian was a supremely skilled interviewer. On the occasion of Bill's visit to the guest spot, rain started to fall during the break . . .

Normally 'A View from the Boundary' started immediately after the summary of the morning's play and continued until we returned to the studio for the lunchtime scores in the county matches being played around the country – around twenty minutes in all. With rain falling steadily at Leeds, and in the absence of any change of plans indicated by the producer, Brian and Bill continued their chat . . . Bill was in absolutely tremendous form. He impersonated every one of the *Dad's Army* characters, with snatches of dialogue, and the interview stretched further and further into the afternoon.

All the other members of the *TMS* commentary team had returned to the box and were hugely entertained, as, I am sure, were listeners to Radio 3 all over the country. It was a brilliant performance by both Bill and Brian and they both must have been nearly exhausted by the time we changed the subject and gave them a rest.

It was very much one of those occasions when people wrote to say, 'We like it best when rain stops play . . .' That is exactly what the rest of us thought as we sat listening to two superb pros working together.

4

===

Sir Donald George Bradman

In the judgment of most cricket-lovers, Don Bradman is the greatest batsman the world has seen. His Test average of 99.94 is more than 30 runs per innings higher than any other batsman; on his four tours of England he averaged 98.66 (1930), 84.16 (1934), 115.66 (1938) and 89.92 (1948, when he was in his fortieth year). To take the wicket of Don Bradman was the ultimate accolade of any bowler in any country – and in his final Test innings in England (14 August 1948) he was bowled by Eric Hollies, the Warwickshire leg-spinner, second ball, in front of a huge and emotional crowd. A score of only 4 would have given him a Test aggregate of 7,000 runs and an average of 100.

My first glimpse of the great man was in 1948, and in some ways it was a disappointment. I must hastily explain that as a seventeen-year-old I had already been called up to the Yorkshire nets, and there seemed to be just a faint possibility that I might play against the tourists because of injuries to our senior seam bowlers. It would have been – and the thought remains in my mind today – the greatest thrill of my life, and I would have absolutely *loved* to bowl at him, but it was not to be: Ron Aspinall recovered his fitness and the teenager from South Yorkshire was not required.

So I took a day off and went to watch the match at what was, after all, my home ground because I was a member of the Sheffield club. It was an unforgettable occasion. The ground was packed, and after an early wicket, Bradman slowly made his way to the middle. The entire crowd rose to its feet and applauded him every step of the way, just as the spectators at The Oval were to do later in the season. Little did I dream at that moment that I would one day shake The Don's hand and, in fact, become a personal friend. It was sufficient that I was seeing the legend in action on his last tour of England.

He got 86 runs in the second innings and then was out, caught Hutton bowled Aspinall, and I shall never forget the next few incredible minutes. The whole crowd rose and booed the bowler! They had come to see Don Bradman and, to a man, they wanted to see him make a hundred.

This generosity of spirit is not unprecedented in Yorkshire. There have been one or two young bowlers – particularly in the Bradford League where so many county players have originated – who have dismissed the visiting pro and been rewarded with such shouts as: 'We've come to see 'im, not *thee*.' They had paid their money at the gate and they wanted their tanner's worth.

I knew how those people felt as I sat in the pavilion, about three places from the aisle, as Bradman walked back and up the steps and disappeared from the gaze of me and the Yorkshire crowd for ever. As if we hadn't seen enough of him in the past eighteen years – he scored 334 in 1930, 304 in 1934, 103 in 1938 and 173 not out in 1948, all at Headingley. Bradman's batting may have been a cherished memory to cricket-lovers all over the world, but to Yorkshiremen he was something very special. They had had ample evidence of this on each of his tours.

In 1953 Bradman returned, accompanying Lindsay Hassett's tour and writing a series of articles for the *Daily Mail*. At Lord's I was at last introduced to him and my first impression was surprise at his modest build. I think this is a childhood thing – we expect to find all our heroes to be of heroic stature, don't we? Bradman wasn't a big man by any means, however, for all the ferocious power with which he hit the ball.

Naturally enough, in the conversation that followed, I addressed him as 'Sir Donald', but after the first couple of times I had done this he put his hand on my shoulder and said, 'The name is Don. Call me Don,' so I did. Of course, we were at Lord's and it just had to happen . . .

Within minutes, one of the MCC hierarchy had asked me to step aside for a moment and rebuked me, 'You do realise, don't you, that you should be addressing him as "Sir Donald"?'

I was livid. 'That is exactly what I did after being introduced,' I retorted, 'and it was the man himself who corrected me. He *told* me to call him, simply, Don. Truly great men don't have to ram their titles down your throat. It's people like you who need to be corrected.' Once again, I was in trouble at Lord's. It wasn't the first time, and it wouldn't be the last.

I am glad to say, however that with Sir Donald it has always been 'Don', ever since that time. In Sydney, the first phone call I used to make was to Harold Larwood; in Brisbane the first call was always to Ray Lindwall; and in Adelaide I still call on The Don to see how he is.

I have always found Don affable and courteous, a wonderful man. There are, of course, criticisms of Bradman; I have always found them difficult to credit, and put them down to jealousy of the man and his great reputation. His figures are around 30 runs per Test innings ahead of any other man who ever played, and reflect his sheer genius.

Essentially Don is a modest man, notwithstanding all his achievements. He is quite willing to talk about cricket – loves to do so, in fact – but never have I heard from him a single word which was immodest. He had nothing but the most tremendous respect for men like Harold Larwood, Wally Hammond, Len Hutton, Alec Bedser and, on his own side, for players of the calibre of Stan McCabe, Bill O'Reilly and Lindwall and Miller. This is something I often mull over, and I believe it is one of the major differences between modern players and those of earlier vintage – the respect that great players had for each other.

One of the greatest pleasures of my life was recording a TV interview with Don for the BBC, at a time when he would not be interviewed by *anyone*. The BBC asked me to try, and when I put it to him he said, 'For you, Freddie, certainly.'

So we went along to his home, set up all the paraphernalia, and talked wonderful cricket talk. I noticed a fine oil painting of him by, I think, D'Arcy Doyle, and I asked him where it was done.

'It's painted from a photograph,' he said, 'during an innings at The Oval. I had heard the view of Percy Fender that "Bradman wasn't quite as good as many people thought" so I thought I would just show him.' (He got a double hundred.)

Don has always been reluctant to discuss the Bodyline series, but I eventually got him to talk about it by mentioning the theory of Fender and Jardine that he tended to get a little bit outside the line of the leg-stump facing Larwood. Their view was that perhaps he was just a trifle frightened of Larwood's pace.

'Oh no,' said Bradman. 'I wasn't frightened of Larwood. I honestly don't think I have ever been *frightened* of any bowler. But the field-placing for leg-theory bowling was such that there was a danger of being out to a catch almost anywhere on the leg-side. On the other hand, there were gaps all over the off-side of the field and the only way I could get runs there was by moving away a little to leg to make room for the stroke.'

'You seemed to get into position very quickly indeed,' I said to him, and he agreed. This, above all, was probably the hallmark of Bradman's genius. He was at all times concerned with getting into a position *to score runs*, not merely to play the delivery defensively. Like all great batsmen, he didn't want to do a lot of running – fours was the way to accumulate runs in a long innings.

'I have noticed,' I said, 'in old newsreel films of you batting, that your back foot was often across and beyond the off-stump before the bowler had delivered the ball.'

The Don said, 'Yes . . .'

'But the bowler then still often dropped it short,' I went on. 'Well, I wouldn't have done that. I would have pushed in the yorker.'

'Yes,' said Bradman, 'I have no doubt that you would have done. I've watched you bowl many times and – there's no doubt about it – you were a *thinking* bowler and you watched the batsman, as a good bowler does.'

I had the pleasure of playing golf with Sir Donald and, even in his seventies, his competitive spirit burned like a furnace. He was concerned about beating his opponent but he was also very much concerned with going round in fewer strokes than his age. It's only a few years ago, when he was eighty-four years old, that he went round the golf course in eighty-one strokes.

Fairly recently, I turned up at a golf course to play him, and

was surprised to find he had grown a moustache since I last saw him. I mentioned this and he laughed.

'Oh, that has been forced upon me a bit,' he said. 'I got a couple of nasty mosquito bites on the upper lip which made it difficult to shave, so I have had to let the moustache grow for a bit.'

Despite his age, however, the wicked sense of humour is still there. Only two or three years ago he was asked by a newspaperman, 'How do you think you would have fared against today's bowlers, Sir Donald? Your career average was ninety-nine in Tests; what do you think it would have been against modern bowling and field-placing?'

Bradman pondered the point for a moment, then replied, 'I think I might have averaged about thirty-eight or thirty-nine perhaps.'

The reporter was shaken. 'Do you mean,' he asked breathlessly, 'that you regard today's bowling as so much better?'

'Oh no,' said Sir Donald. 'What you asked was what do I think I would have averaged *today*, and the answer is thirty-eight or thirty-nine. Don't forget that *today* I am eighty-four years old.'

Everyone on the 1962 MCC tour to Australia was thrilled when Sir Robert Menzies persuaded Sir Donald to turn out for the Prime Minister's XI for the one-day fixture in Canberra. He walked out to bat in his baggy green cap, with that same confident air about him that I had seen in Sheffield ten years earlier. He was then fifty years old and it was as if the whole of Australia was there. It was such a wonderful occasion that I can never recall one like it. Such was the legend of Don Bradman. Today, in his late eighties, Don still finds it difficult to walk down a street in Australia without being stopped by members of the public.

I never did get to bowl at him. Nevertheless, I have my friendship with the man, and that is more precious than I can say. On the last Australian tour to this country a man from Adelaide came to the commentary box at Old Trafford and said, 'Mr Trueman, I've been told to deliver this to you personally.' It was a photograph of Bradman playing with his local team in South Australia, and is signed, 'To my great friend, Freddie – Don Bradman.'

That will do for me.

5

Harold Larwood

'Devastating' right-arm fast bowler, as he is described in the Who's Who *of Cricketers, which goes on to add, 'Controversy and ill-feeling reduced the career of Larwood, regarded as the greatest fast bowler of the inter-war period, to just over six years.' In fact he played in only twenty-one Tests and his international career was effectively ended by the 1932–3 tour by England to Australia. The controversy arose because of England's policy of 'leg-theory', which the Australians renamed Bodyline, a definition which is now generally applied in both countries. Larwood's contribution to that tour was 33 Test wickets at 19.51, enabling England to win the series by four matches to one. However, he never again played for his country.*

My first encounter with Harold Larwood came during the 1958–9 tour to Australia and my reaction was one of astonishment at the slight stature of the man whose name had become synonymous with the most hostile of fast bowling. I was less than two years old when Larwood was bowling on the Bodyline tour, creating a controversy which stretched across the world, and almost caused a complete break in Commonwealth (or Imperial, as they were at the time) relations. Even as a very small boy indeed, I became aware of these events.

Yet here was this man, almost a frail figure it seemed, joining us in the England dressing-room in Sydney, in January 1959. He was fifty-four years old, and I know that the human body is supposed to diminish as we grow older, but looking at the slight build and frame of this little, grey-haired man I still found it difficult to believe that here was a figure who had terrorised Australian batsmen with his sheer pace. Well, *some* Australian batsmen, I should say: he did not have that effect on Don Bradman, as some people would have us believe. Harold Larwood himself told me this – not once but many times. He had nothing but the highest professional respect for The Don and never at any time did I ever hear him waver in that view. Bradman, remember, averaged just under 50 in the Bodyline series, but it is the view of the opposition which counts, far more than any statistics.

My first meeting with Larwood in Sydney was in some ways historic. Harold became depressed and disillusioned by his exclusion from Test cricket after 1932–3, and had no intention of watching our series of 1958–9 in Australia, where he went to live in 1949. Cricket had given nothing to Harold, and left him with a fund of bitter memories.

Larwood's move to Australia was, in itself, perhaps a bit surprising: so sharp was the bitterness caused by the Bodyline tour that Australia is the last place one would have expected Larwood to settle. However, he enjoyed life in Australia – though he could never get used to the idea that the Prime Minister could (and often did) walk unaccompanied down a public street and stop to chat to people on the way. He had grown up with the idea that Prime Ministers are a bit more remote than that. I believe the move was arranged by Jack Fingleton, the former opening batsman who became a very fine journalist, and that great Prime Minister, Sir Robert Menzies.

So here he was, this slight man whose bowling had caused such extreme controversy, now persuaded to come and look at some

Test cricket again only by a personal approach from George Duckworth, the former Lancashire and England wicket-keeper who, in 1958–9, was our scorer and baggage-master. He had played with and against Harold, knew him well and was able to talk him into coming to the game.

I was fascinated to meet the man about whom I had heard so much. I was also very interested to learn that he came from a village only twenty-odd miles or so from where I was born. (I was so nearly qualified to play for Notts!) We became friends very quickly and we remained friends until Harold died. After that first thrilling meeting, I visited Larwood's home in Sydney many times.

There have been many versions of the Bodyline story told over the years – theories, opinions, accusations and counter-accusations, bad feeling and outright enmity. This is the Larwood version as he personally told it to me in the course of many conversations.

It all began, according to Larwood, when Notts played Middlesex at Lord's during the summer of 1932. During the tea interval one day, the Notts captain, Arthur Carr, said to Larwood and his new-ball partner Bill Voce, 'I don't know what you two have got planned for this evening but I want you to have dinner with me.' The two bowlers looked at each other, surprised in the extreme. Professionals didn't dine with amateurs in those days; they didn't even stay in the same hotel as each other.

However, off they went to a West End restaurant – the sort of place neither of them could afford to patronise – and were shown to a curtained alcove. When the curtain was drawn back, Larwood and Voce were astonished to find Percy Fender and Douglas Jardine sitting there. The party enjoyed their meal, and when it was finished and the crockery removed, the condiments were left behind along with one or two other things, to serve, as it turned out, as symbols. It was on that tabletop that England's leg-theory attack was conceived and developed.

Jardine (who would be captain in Australia the following winter) had an almost obsessional desire to win back the Ashes, which had been lost in the summer of 1930. He didn't like Australians and, in particular, he didn't like Bradman. Jardine and Fender pointed out that during the 1930 tour they had noticed that as Larwood had run in to bowl, Bradman had edged slightly away outside the leg-stump, as though there was a hint of nervousness.

As Harold was telling me this story, twenty-five years later, it occurred to me that someone must have had remarkably good eyesight. Fender and Jardine didn't play in the 1930 Test series, so they could not have observed Bradman at particularly close quarters. In any case, Bradman's scores in the 1930 series were 8 and 131, 254 and 1, 334, 14, and 232. Bradman's aggregate was 974 runs and his average was 139.14. He didn't seem to have done much backing away on those figures.

Larwood was even more emphatic about it. He had told Fender and Jardine, 'I didn't notice him backing away and he certainly wasn't afraid. Bradman is afraid of no bowler.' However, the two amateurs insisted on having their way.

The leg-theory was tried out in the match between the county champions v. The Rest – and it didn't work! Leg-theory was smashed all round The Oval. This didn't seem to put anyone off, however, and the theory was discussed in detail during the sea voyage to Australia, although it wasn't used in the First Test. Bradman was ill and missed the match, and leg-theory had been devised with Bradman very much in mind.

Bradman returned for the Second Test, in Melbourne, and all Australia waited for a repeat of his great deeds of the 1930 tour to England. It was then that Bill Bowes bowled The Don, first ball.

Dear old Bill used to tell the story with great dramatic detail: 'The crowd applauded him all the way to the wicket, then, just as I was about to run in, the applause rose again in a great crescendo. When silence descended again, I prepared to bowl – and it was *complete* silence. You could hear the clattering

of the trams down in Flinders Street. Suddenly I realised that
Bradman was expecting me to bowl a bouncer . . . and to use
the leg-theory. I signalled to fine-leg to come up a bit – to
strengthen the illusion that a bouncer was coming – and ran
in. I saw Bradman start to get into position for the bouncer –
and let him have a good-length ball. Even then, he was good
enough to change his position, and he *almost* managed to play
it – but not quite. And the man all Australia had been waiting to
see murder the English bowling was out, bowled, first ball. The
silence, as he walked back to the pavilion, continued. Then, one
spectator – just one – started to clap again . . .'

Bill told the story wonderfully in that breathless voice of his.
Listening to it, you were taken out into the middle with him at
the massive Melbourne Cricket Ground.

Bradman hadn't finished with England, however, not by any
means. In the second innings he scored 103 not out – in a total
of 191 – and Australia won by 111 runs.

One of Larwood's outstanding memories of that tour had
nothing to do with bowling at all. In the last Test, in Sydney,
he went in as nightwatchman, and the following day got to
98. A Test century was almost within his grasp when he was
caught by a chap called Ironmonger.

'I don't think,' said Harold, 'he had ever held a catch
in his life up to that point, and he had to save it for
me!'

How, then, did Larwood himself get on with Aussies? He
felt the hostility and resentment of the public during that
series, but never held it against them, understanding why they
felt that way. Once he had emigrated there, however, sixteen
or seventeen years after the Bodyline series, he settled down
well. There was no nastiness towards him until *that* film was
made, in Australia, about the Bodyline series, and then, said
Harold he got one or two nasty letters. He couldn't help feeling
amused, though, at the way the film portrayed the Australian
players as smartly dressed individuals and the England men as
ill-mannered, scruffy louts!

One of the main characteristics of Larwood's style was not just his tremendous pace, but his brilliant accuracy, which was why he was chosen for the role. He bowled leg-theory because that was what the game-plan demanded.

So important was Larwood to Jardine's campaign that even when he injured his foot he was ordered to stay on the field. It happened in Sydney, in the last Test.

'Sorry, Captain, but I shall have to go off,' he said to his skipper.

'Stay where you are,' demanded Jardine. 'You will not leave the field until I say so.'

'But I'm injured,' protested Larwood. 'Suppose I have to run after the ball? I shan't be able to do it.'

'Stay on the field,' said Jardine. And there Larwood remained until Hedley Verity bowled Bradman for 71. 'Now you can go off for treatment,' said the captain.

It has to be remembered that discipline in those days was absolute, and professionals did not argue with amateurs. There was an almost feudal relationship between the players, and the foot-soldier, the professional, did as he was told. It was all very, very different back then.

Harold insisted until the end of his days that during the Bodyline tour he was merely following orders in an era when you did as the captain instructed. He didn't want to hurt anybody – I'm convinced of that – but Jardine had decided on a method which *he* felt would be too much for the Aussies. Well, it wasn't too much for Bradman, that's for sure.

What really sickened Larwood was not the hostility of the Australians – he could understand the reason for that – it was the attitude back home. No one seemed to regard Jardine as in any way responsible (at least as Harold saw it). All the anger seemed to be directed at Larwood. The last straw came when his own county drew up a letter of apology for his part in the Bodyline tour and asked him to sign it.

Let me make this clear: Harold Larwood was a very *proud* man. He took pride in playing for his county and for his country,

but, more than that, he was proud of his working-class roots, proud of his background and of his family. When that letter of apology was shown to him he was stunned. He spoke to his parents about it and was told in no uncertain terms that he would be no son of theirs if he signed it.

Harold, I know, had seen it all coming. He did not go on to New Zealand when the Australian tour ended, but took the boat back home. This gave him plenty of time to reflect on the stir which had been caused, and gradually he realised that he was the one who would receive the major share of blame for what had happened. He just couldn't understand this: all he had done was back up his captain with a hundred per cent loyalty, no more than that.

The terrible analogy became clear later: the generals set up something unpleasant; the troops followed orders; and the foot-soldiers were the ones who got the blame for it all. It left Larwood feeling very bitter.

Harold came back to England three or four times on visits and was now welcomed into the Notts committee room at Trent Bridge by a much more enlightened body of men, but he was a sad man. You could see it in his eyes and hear it in his voice as he spoke. This treatment by the Establishment is something I have never been able to understand.

On every visit to Australia I called to see Harold, and we talked and talked. What always staggered me was that this great bowler, this English cricketing hero, lived in near poverty on his little bit of a pension. He even gave up smoking because he could no longer afford to buy cigarettes.

He lost most of his sight towards the end. The last time we met, he signed four bats for me with difficulty, and gave me a book which he also signed. I remember saying to my wife after that meeting, 'The old boy is fading a bit. I do hope he is still here the next time we come to Australia.'

Sadly, about eighteen months later I learned that the legend had died. Larwood's name will live on, however. He is part of cricket history – a very big part.

Harold left me with one sobering thought: 'Freddie,' he said, 'you are a truly great fast bowler, but there's just one problem – you are not hostile enough.' Well, there are one or two people who might not agree with that, but who am I to argue with the master?

6

===

George Herbert Hirst and Wilfred Rhodes

These two incomparable all-rounders, whose achievements put modern practitioners completely in the shade, made up two-thirds of what was known, in the period around the turn of the twentieth century, as 'the Huddersfield Triumvirate'. The third member was Schofield Haigh, a good fast-medium bowler, who was a useful enough batsman to pile up 11,715 runs in his career and to play in eleven Tests for England, but never reached the same pinnacle of immortality as the other two. I never met Schofield Haigh, who died ten years before I was born, so it is of the other two that I shall write.

In 1948, as a boy of seventeen, I was invited to the Yorkshire nets for special coaching as one of the county's promising youngsters. I arrived at Headingley with my father, who found himself a seat behind the indoor nets while I changed in the old dressing-rooms and walked across to the indoor shed which now has hospitality boxes perched on top of it.

I was greeted by a little old man with a sheet of paper

who asked my name, checked it against his list and said,
'Oh yes. Fast bowler. You have been recommended by Mr
Cyril Turner.' (Cyril was the former Yorkshire all-rounder
of the 1930s who later became the county's scorer and also
acted as a talent-spotting scout in South Yorkshire.) My identity
established, I was then asked to let them see me bowl. I marked
out a run-up and I think I bowled a total of five deliveries before
the old gentleman stopped me.

'Where were you born?' he asked.

I replied, 'A place called Scotch Springs, Stainton.'

'And what's the nearest town?' he went on.

'It will be Doncaster, or perhaps Rotherham,' I answered.

'Right,' said this chap. 'Are you on your own or has anyone
come with you?' I answered that my dad was with me, sitting
behind the nets. 'Take me over to him,' he said, so off I went
and introduced him to my father. I still had no idea who the little
old man was, but my father knew. He sat up as if somebody had
shot him in the behind.

'Put your coat on,' was my next instruction, 'and sit over
'ere,' and with that George Herbert Hirst and my father
disappeared.

When they returned, about an hour and a half later, it turned
out that they had been checking the exact geographical location
of Scotch Springs . . . to make sure it was actually in Yorkshire.
There might have been no hard and fast rule, nothing actually
in writing, about Yorkshire CCC players having to be born
within the county, but no one at the time stood a chance if
he had been born *outside* the boundaries. My father had been
checked, and my birthplace had been double-checked. I crept
in by a matter of a few hundred yards, otherwise I would have
been a Nottinghamshire man!

It was only when we were going home on the train that I
learned I had been questioned, then watched in the nets, by
none other than George Herbert Hirst, one of Yorkshire's
legends. I was amazed by how small and frail he seemed to me.
I suppose, on reflection, I expected a man whose achievements

were monumental to be some kind of heroic figure. This man had scored 2,000 runs and taken 200 wickets in one season (1906), which must have involved an unbelievable effort of graft as well as a high degree of skill. He also did the double (1,000 runs and 100 wickets in a season) fourteen times. He was a left-arm, medium-fast, over-the-wicket bowler, known in his day as a 'swerve' bowler (or 'swing', as it is known today). And this was the little old man who had welcomed me to Headingley . . .

Hirst, in later years, taught me things which, up to that point, I had never dreamed about: that a bowler must not only observe an opposing batsman closely, but he must particularly watch his feet . . . always watch his first movement.

One occasion I remember with absolute clarity. We were playing against Warwickshire at Huddersfield and for some reason I could not explain, I had (temporarily, I fervently hoped!) lost the ability to move the ball away from a right-hand batsman. I simply could not work out what had gone wrong. During the luncheon interval I was sitting in the dressing-room when George Hirst came in and asked why I was no longer bowling the outswinger. I had to confess that I simply didn't know and couldn't explain it.

'It's nowt,' he consoled me. 'We can put it right while we're sat 'ere. When you deliver t'ball you're breaking your wrist and dropping it. That's all that's t'matter,' and he demonstrated, there and then, exactly what he meant.

Believe it or not, I went out that afternoon and did as Hirst had suggested, and suddenly I was swinging the ball again. Here was a man who must have been eighty years of age at the time, sitting in the stands and watching me from a hundred yards' distance – and he had spotted what I was doing wrong with my wrist!

All his life Hirst had the most marvellous eye, and this was especially true when he was assessing other cricketers. I've already mentioned that I had bowled only about five deliveries in the nets before he had seen enough. I was told that when he went to look at Len Hutton as a very young man, he watched for only two overs before announcing, 'Sign him up. We've got a worldbeater.'

I spent a long time talking cricket to him whenever I got the chance. In the 1950s I was amazed that we were not winning the county championship with men like Hutton, Appleyard, Wardle, Yardley, Close, Lowson, Brennan behind the stumps, and I asked Hirst about the great Yorkshire team round about the turn of the century and others into the 1920s and 1930s.

He told me, 'In those days, basically there were only three sides that had to be beaten – Lancashire, Middlesex and Surrey – unless something went seriously wrong. If we beat them once, and drew t'other game against 'em, we could generally expect to win t'championship.'

'And against other counties, did you really only book into a hotel for two nights?' I asked.

'Oh yes,' he said, without a trace of arrogance. 'There was no need to bother ourselves about Somerset, or Hampshire,

or Essex or Derbyshire and t'rest. We just had to be sure of winning at least once against them three.'

Looking back on those conversations with him, it's interesting to recall that we spent hours 'talking cricket' in great detail. In the 1950s and 1960s 'my' Yorkshire side did the same thing. Younger players sat on the outskirts of these discussions – I like to think in respectful silence – and they *learned*. After the sixties, that sort of cricket forum virtually ceased, and it might be seen as significant that Yorkshire have never won the county championship since that time.

George Hirst told me about the hours, the days, he spent in winter trying to improve his bowling. He was, basically, a medium-paced bowler who made the ball swing *in* to the batsman, and he decided that to beat the *great* players of his day he had to develop the one that went away from the right-hander. The day came when he took the wicket of the great Jack Hobbs with the outswinger, and the rumour goes that a letter of complaint was received by Yorkshire at the ungentlemanly conduct of George Hirst in deceiving Hobbs in such an underhand manner! Stories do get embellished as the years go by. Only last year a *Daily Telegraph* cricket writer credited me with having said to a young university batsman, 'Aye, it were wasted on thee,' when congratulated on a particularly good delivery which had disposed of the batsman. That was certainly said, and to a university batsman, but it was said by Emmott Robinson – before I was born!

George Hirst was a truly great cricketer and a wonderfully kind and considerate man. His equally great – probably greater – contemporary, Wilfred Rhodes, came from exactly the same part of Huddersfield (Kirkheaton), but he was an entirely different sort of character. Hirst and Schofield Haigh were genial souls who spent hours playing practical jokes on each other. One cannot think of Wilfred Rhodes indulging in capers of that kind. Cricket was a very serious business indeed to him and there was no place in the game for jokes. But what a player: fractionally under 40,000 runs and well over 4,000 wickets . . .

the double on sixteen occasions, more than any other man . . .
2,000 runs and 100 wickets in a season twice . . . the records
just go on and on. Don't talk to me about post-Second World
War players when you talk about great all-rounders – look
no further than Wilfred Rhodes. At Test level, he started as
a number eleven batsman, and in 1903–4 he figured in the
record last-wicket partnership of 130 with Reginald Foster;
less than ten years later he was opening the batting and
shared the *first*-wicket record partnership of 323 with Jack
Hobbs!

Rhodes actually played first-class cricket for thirty-two years,
and as no one is likely to do that again his records are destined
to stand for all time. He was an intense sort of character: grim,
almost taciturn. Knowing him in his later years it was not
difficult to picture him as a young man, teaching himself how
to bowl, alone in a barn, hour after hour. His patience must
have been monumental. Can anyone imagine the self-discipline
it must have taken to bowl for hours on end, with chalk-marks
on the ball so as to observe how it behaved through the air and
off the pitch; retrieving the ball himself after every delivery? It
must have seemed like one of the labours of Hercules.

Rhodes was fifty-two years old when he bowled for the last
time – at Scarborough, where he had begun his first-class career
– and saw Bradman dropped by Bob Wyatt, first ball. He was
as livid as he would have been if it had been the first ball he
ever bowled. This great man had started by bowling at Grace,
and he finished by bowling at Bradman. Can there ever have
been more wonderful parameters to a cricketing life?

It was at Scarborough that he used to sit and 'watch' cricket
long after his sight had failed. He would listen to the sound of
bat on ball and remark, 'That was a good 'un . . . right off the
middle,' or 'that wor an edge, worn't it? Where's it gone?' He
actually followed the course of play by the *sound*. If there was
any detail he somehow failed to grasp he'd ask. I can see him
now, sitting in front of the pavilion at Scarborough and trying
his damnedest to follow every detail of the play. I used to sit with

him and provide the occasional guidance, but he liked to work it out for himself if it was at all possible. An amazing man.

His eyesight actually started to go while he was still playing, but he couldn't bring himself to retire. He is alleged to have said, 'You know, I've tried on every pair of glasses in Woolworth's but I couldn't get one that helped.' I suppose you could buy a pair in Woolworth's at that time for twopence or threepence and Rhodes had tried the whole stock, rather than go to an optician. Oh, he was a good Yorkshireman, all right, as well as an outstanding cricketer!

Rhodes must have been seventy when he was asked to open a new cricket ground in the Bradford League – I think it was at Bingley – and I was invited along as well. After the opening ceremony he bowled a delivery or two off a couple of paces. So I did see him bowl, this great man who had bowled at Grace and who had bowled at Bradman.

One incident almost led me to believe he was invested with

superhuman powers. I was sitting with him at a Festival game at Scarborough when he asked to go to the toilet. I took him by the arm and led him to the appropriate quarters, and while we were standing there he suddenly said, 'Cowdrey's out.' I couldn't believe my ears, and led him back to his seat in a sort of daze. It was only then that I realised he had changed his usual habits and was listening to the radio commentary on the game through an earpiece attached to a little transistor wireless set in his pocket.

To sit and listen to Rhodes talk about cricket was a unique experience. It took a bit to get him going and he hadn't much time for anybody who didn't know what he was talking about. He was, and remained, a hundred per cent absorbed in the game for the whole of his life. Of course, the legends built up, as they have always done around the great names of the game.

One of the classics of this genre involves the 1902 Oval Test, when Rhodes, as England's number eleven, joined Hirst with 15 runs needed for victory. Hirst allegedly said to him, 'We'll get 'em in singles.'

It's a nice romantic tale, the sort that abounds in cricket. Wilfred Rhodes always denied that anything of the kind was ever said, however. My friend Don Mosey actually tape-recorded an interview with Wilfred in which he denied, absolutely, that any such remark was ever made, and printed that denial in a book called *We Don't Play It for Fun* in 1988.

The story came up again as recently as February 1997, when a man wrote to the *Daily Telegraph* to say that no Yorkshireman would ever have said 'singles', but would have said 'wooons'. Well, we have the word of Wilfred Rhodes that George Herbert Hirst never said anything of the kind to him. It's the sort of story which we would *like* to be true, as there are too many of the other sort kicking around, and I have suffered from more than my fair share of them myself. There are enough good *true* stories about cricketers to make it unnecessary to invent new ones.

I asked Wilfred what it was like to play under the captaincy of Lord Hawke, another Yorkshire cricket legendary figure, but not known, perhaps, as much for his playing ability as his autocratic attitude. 'Oh aye,' Rhodes said, 'he was a very nice man.' Then, a bit to my surprise, he added, 'And he was a very good captain.'

'Was he?' I asked, probably sounding doubtful.

'Oh yes. He did as he wor told. We used to tell 'im to go to mid-off or mid-on while we could get in close and do a bit o' nattering.'

Can't you just picture the scene? The amateur, patrician captain standing alone at mid-on while Hirst, Rhodes and the rest crowded close to the wicket and discussed what to do next? I certainly can.

His Lordship (as the old players always respectfully referred to their leader) was 'a good captain' in ways that mattered to his grizzled professionals. Don't forget that in 'the good old days' the captain would join the committee for luncheon, while the pros ate the sandwiches they had brought to the ground and, perhaps, take a pint of beer whilst mingling with the general public in the bar! It was Lord Hawke who changed all that and insisted that the 'players' be served with lunch like the amateurs.

Rhodes' thoughts never strayed far from the technical aspects of his game. 'Australians are good cricketers,' he once mentioned to me. 'Aye . . . good players. Always have a look how they hold t'bat, and when you're bowling, try to keep away from leg-and-middle. You'll find that Australians grip the bat with t'right 'and low on the 'andle. That's why they're good on-side players. Keep to about off-and-middle and make t'ball go away from 'em and you'll 'ave less bother with 'em.'

I once asked him if he got most of his wickets in any particular fashion, and he astonished me by saying he got a lot 'caught at that third man position by bowling the one that bounced a bit'. I've never been able to work that one out, but I do know, from reports of his field-placing, that he always bowled with a long-on and long-off – presumably offering a challenge to hit him over the top.

Peter Parfitt tells of an occasion at Scarborough when he was sitting with Rhodes, and Don Wilson was bowling slow left-arm for Yorkshire. Rhodes asked what the field-setting was, and was appalled that there was a deep square-leg. Parfitt mentioned that Wilson was also bowling with a leg-slip, ten or eleven yards back, and the old man nodded, commenting, 'Aye, 'e's balling too straight. He wants to get more ower to off-and-middle.'

He was then approaching ninety years of age, and the old cricket brain was still ticking over, still analysing, still picturing the scene. It was in moments like that it became less difficult to see him as a young man, bowling for hour after hour by himself in that barn, retrieving the ball after each delivery, thinking about what had just happened, plotting what to do next.

Rhodes earned every word of the tribute from Jim Kilburn, the elegant essayist of the *Yorkshire Post*: 'Every over of Rhodes was a creation of beauty. There was no crudity, no self-consciousness, no striving for effect. Rhodes bowled always with the maturity of the practised husbandman scything corn, all the effort and patience and unbroken rhythm. He might have bowled unsuccessfully but he never bowled badly.'

Neville Cardus, reporting a Roses match of 1926, wrote in the *Manchester Guardian*: '. . . Rhodes bowling his beautifully curved flight. The man's action is just as it always has been these many years: easy and masterful. History hangs about him – the legendary Rhodes. Men who are playing with him in this match were not born when he first came to us, the greatest of our slow bowlers – only a youth with an innocent, unrazored face.' Wonderful prose to describe a wonderful man.

I never tired of those magical occasions when I sat and listened to him. On the contrary, I treasured every second of them. I find it inexpressibly sad that today's players will run a mile rather than listen to their elders. The stock reply, if they are forced into a corner and have to offer one, is, 'Oh, it's a different game today.' It is indeed, but it isn't a better one.

Hirst and Rhodes . . . wonderful, wonderful men and cricketers. We shall never see players like them again, and there can be no greater pity than that.

7

Maurice Leyland, Arthur Mitchell and Others

Mitchell and Leyland, as the Yorkshire CCC coaches when their playing days were over, worked superbly in harness, yet were as dissimilar as individuals as Hirst and Rhodes before them. Leyland was friendly, genial, smiling; Mitchell grim and taciturn. Both were magnificent coaches, but achieved their results in different ways. There is no doubt, however, that they were both characters in the most colourful sense, as were one or two others around before them.

First, we must talk about Maurice Leyland as a player – and a fine player he was. Walter Robins told me about a team discussion before the First Test on the 1936–7 tour to Australia. When it came to Maurice's turn to put in his four-penn'orth, he had this to say: 'Now this feller Bradman – I can't do owt about 'im. That's a matter for t'bowlers. But Bill O'Reilly's bowling is summat else. You just leave 'im to me cos I've

got 'im skinned.' To prove his point, he went out next day
and scored 126, which remained the only century scored by
an Englishman at The Gabba for nearly forty years.

O'Reilly is regarded by most Australians and many English-
men, too, as the greatest leg-spinner of all time, and there is little
doubt that he troubled most English batsmen in his day. Leyland
seemed always to have his measure, however. Many years later I
was sitting at a Test match with Len Hutton. O'Reilly was only a
few yards away, in front of the pavilion, an interested spectator
some time after he had retired. 'Go and ask that feller what he
thinks of Maurice Leyland,' said Len.

I didn't do that, but I did ask Maurice how he came to get
the better of Bill. He said, 'I don't know really. It might have
been that the first ball he ever bowled to me was a googly –
don't ask me why. I never seemed to have any bother with 'im
after that.'

Whatever the reason, Leyland remains possibly the only
Yorkshire-born batsman who could cope with that type of
bowling for many years. It was always reckoned in my time,
for instance, that Yorkshiremen could not play leg-spinners at
all, but it's a fact that Maurice Leyland usually got the better
of one of the best there has ever been.

Maurice had a lovely, gentle sense of humour. Once, batting
in a Test at Lord's, he was comprehensively bowled by a
delivery which knocked two stumps out of the ground. As
he turned to walk back to the pavilion he glanced down at
the stumps and then, on impulse, plucked out the one which
remained standing and laid it beside the other two. This, of
course, did not pass without notice. A ripple of laughter ran
round the ground, but there was no answering smile from the
selectors. After Maurice had unbuckled his pads a message came
that he was wanted in the committee room, so he put on his
blazer and sauntered off to see why he had been summoned.
He was asked, sternly, by the selectors, why he had removed
the last stump.

Maurice gave this his earnest consideration for a minute, then

George Hirst, a man with an unerring instinct for spotting talent.

Wilfred Rhodes. On figures alone he has to be the greatest of all-rounders.

Maurice Leyland, a much-loved character with a great sense of humour.

Walter Hammond had an insatiable appetite for runs – and for wickets and catches.

The tall figure of Percy Chapman stands out in the 1928 MCC side at the Scarborough Festival. Left to right; George Macaulay, Maurice Leyland, George Geary, Percy Chapman, Wally Hammond, George Duckworth, Ernest Tyldesley, Herbert Sutcliffe, Jack Hobbs, Patsy Hendren, Maurice Tate.

Headley hits out against England in 1939.

George Headley, the black Bradman – or was Bradman the white Headley?

On the way to Australia with no thought of the controversy ahead: Harold Larwood, Bill Voce, Tommy Mitchell and (throwing) Maurice Leyland in 1932.

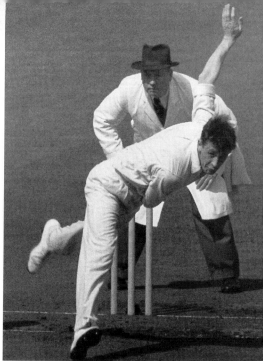

Off to the West Indies in 1953: My old mate and partner, Brian Statham.
Left, top to bottom; Tom Graveney,
Ken Suttle, Reg Spooner, Willie Watson,
Trevor Bailey, Charles Palmer (manager), Len Hutton. Right, top to bottom;
Jim Laker, Tony Lock, Peter May, Brian Statham, F.S.T., Johnny Wardle,
Alan Moss, Godfrey Evans, Denis Compton.

A quartet of Yorkshiremen bound for the West Indies in 1953: Willie Watson,
F.S.T., Johnny Wardle and Len Hutton.

The beautiful bowling action of Ray Lindwall.

Two Yorkshire captains – Brian Sellers (in unusually genial mood) and Norman Yardley.

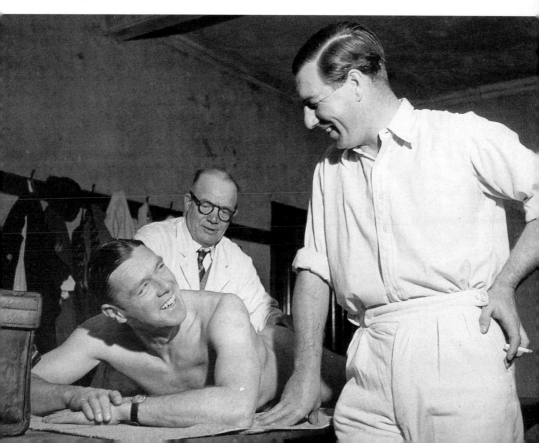

A handsome young John Arlott standing as a parliamentary election candidate.

A thoughtful study of my friend and neighbour Peter Parfitt.

A respectful salute for the Duke of Norfolk and Prince Philip, Duke of Edinburgh.

F.S.T. leads England from the field after taking his 300th Test wicket at The Oval in 1964, with applause led by Ted Dexter, Ken Barrington and Peter Parfitt.

The England team for the 1964 Test against Australia at The Oval: back row, left to right; Peter Parfitt, Jim Parks, Tom Cartwright, John Price, Bob Barber, Geoffrey Boycott, 'Sandy' Taitt (masseur) and Colin Drybrough (12th man). Front row, left to right; Fred Titmus, Colin Cowdrey, Ted Dexter (Captain), F.S.T. and Ken Barrington.

A tearful twosome – Harry Secombe
and friend.

. . . And a smiling twosome – Bill
Maynard and friend.

Tom Graveney and Alec Bedser – two exceptionally talented players.

said, 'Well, d'you know, I thought it looked a bit lonely standing theer by itssen.'

Fielding once on the boundary in a Roses match at Old Trafford, he dropped a catch. There was a moment of stunned silence; it was the sort of incident which could make or ruin the day for a Yorkshireman or a Lancastrian. The ground was packed and the crowd had been allowed to sit behind the boundary ropes, in the corners of the ground. It was one of the spectators there who broke the silence: 'I could have copped that in me mouth,' he jeered.

Leyland, without pausing between picking up the ball and returning it to the wicket-keeper, nodded his agreement. 'Aye, and if my mouth was as big as thine, I'd 'ave done t'same.'

He used to say to me, in his later days as coach, 'Come on, Freddie – you've got to bat better than you do. You've got a good defence and you can play strokes. Why are you always trying to 'it t'ball for six?'

I used to reply, with what I imagined to be innocent simplicity, 'Cos I *like* to hit sixes.' Herbert Sutcliffe and Arthur Mitchell used to say much the same thing to me.

Then Maurice resorted to bribery – or at any rate, a challenge: he bet me four tins of Gold Block tobacco (we were both pipe-smokers) that I couldn't get a 50. When I did, he paid me, with a huge beam of satisfaction. Then I had to get 50 runs and five wickets in an innings . . . and he bought me a pipe. Next, I had to get 50 and ten wickets in a match . . . and for that my reward was to be a stone of humbugs! I think it was at Leeds or Bradford that I managed it.

My next game was at Harrogate, where Maurice lived. He delivered a stone of those big, black and white humbugs to the St George's Road ground, and you have never seen anything like it. I honestly don't know where he had got hold of the sweets, but they were *everywhere*! All the team, plus the scorer and masseur, took some home for their kids. I put some in the car for my youngsters. They had spilled over into the office and John Nash, the secretary, had had a few, but there were still so many left, that I didn't know what to do.

I made a few phone calls and found a children's home which would be glad of the sweets, but the matron asked if I would deliver them personally. So at the end of the day I went there, and in some ways that visit changed my life. There were children in wheelchairs, some able to walk only with sticks, and I thought about how I could run around a cricket field while these children would never have a chance to do anything like that. One little lad, who could only get about with the help of a Zimmer frame, told me he was going to enter a long-distance race – using his frame! It absolutely broke me up, and I had to leave after that. I have always done what I could for children's charities since that day.

When I told Maurice about it, he put an arm round my shoulders and said, 'I know how you feel. You've done your good deed for the day.'

A mixture of kindliness, gentle humour and homespun philosophy, was Maurice Leyland. In my early playing days I once confided in him that I had started making the ball nip back off the seam – at pace – and I didn't know how I was doing it.

Maurice thought for a minute, then gave me this advice: 'If you don't know 'ow it's 'appening, you can be sure t'bloke wi' t'bat 'as no idea – so keep on wi' it.'

Maurice had a favourite pub in Harrogate – I think it was called the New Inn – and I used, when off duty, to go over there and sit and talk to him. Sometimes we went to his club and played snooker, but always, over a game of snooker or a half-pint of beer, we talked cricket. When I eventually got the first of my three centuries I think he was just as delighted as I was.

He loved a laugh, but I've never seen him laugh quite as much as one day in 1954 in the winter nets. Maurice was coaching a left-arm fast bowler called Brian James who kept dropping it short. Patiently, he explained to the bowler that the object of the exercise was to get the ball to swing, and for that to be effective he had to pitch the ball up to the batsman. Brian listened, nodded, and went back to his mark. In he came – and the ball must have slipped out of his hand. It went up and up, out of the nets completely, and was heading for the roof of the shed.

Sitting *behind* the nets and watching it all was T. H. (Tom) Taylor, the Yorkshire president, perched on a shooting-stick. The ball soared up to the roof, and Mr Taylor turned to see where it had gone. As he did so, he toppled forward, bringing down the net! His chauffeur rushed forward to try to rescue him, as both the president and his shooting-stick became completely entangled. Laugh? It was like something out of the furthest realms of slapstick comedy. Maurice collapsed completely on to the floorboards. Never have I seen him laugh as much.

Sadly, Maurice died in 1967. There was a massive turn-out of all the surviving old players at his funeral. I looked at them, grouped together in the church in Harrogate, and reflected on the collective memories they must have . . .

Arthur 'Ticker' Mitchell struck terror into the souls of a hundred youngsters; and undoubtedly he turned a similar number of raw schoolboys into county cricketers. A brilliant coach who never minced his words, he was quite capable of telling a young player (who might have the most cordial recommendation to the nets), 'What's thi job . . . joiner? Well, if I were thee, lad, I'd stick to that and forget all abaht laikin' cricket.' While he could spot talent and potential, he could equally weed out the no-hopers while wondering aloud how they had got that far.

Arthur was a man of dark intensity who always seemed to growl rather than speak. While Maurice Leyland loved to laugh, Arthur Mitchell might manage a grim smile – but not very often. If the occasion arose when praise was called for, the words had to be forced reluctantly from a sparse vocabulary.

He might, of course, have had an entirely different personality at home, amongst his family, but somehow I doubt it. His son Alf, a sound club cricketer with long experience in the Airedale and Wharfedale League, was once chatting about the modern tendency to over-react to the taking of a wicket, by bowler and fieldsmen alike, with much embracing and exchanging of 'high fives'. Someone mischievously asked Alf how 'Ticker' would have viewed the spectacle of one cricketer kissing another.

'D'you know,' he replied thoughtfully, 'I can't even remember him kissing my mother.'

Ellis Robinson, part of the redoubtable close-catching contingent of Yorkshire CCC in the 1930s, dived full length to take a brilliant catch off Verity's bowling and lay, for a moment, on the grass, confidently expecting at least an odd word of congratulation from his colleagues grouped about him. No one uttered a word for a moment and it was Mitchell who finally snarled, through gritted teeth, 'Gerrup. Tha'rt makin' an exhibition o' thissen.'

Another in the same mould was George Macaulay, a fast-medium bowler who played 445 matches for the county in the 1920s and 1930s. Like Mitchell after him, Macaulay liked nothing better than the life-and-death tussle of a Roses match between the wars. There was some suspicion in the Yorkshire camp that one Old Trafford wicket in particular had been under-prepared, with Lancashire gambling on winning the toss and batting first. The gamble came unstuck: Macaulay bowled them out twice, after which he raced over to the pavilion and shouted up to the Lancastrians in the dressing-room, 'Get thi pads on and I'll ball you bastards out again.'

A different type again – a man with a personality all his own – was Emmott Robinson, a man who did not play first-class cricket until he was in his mid-thirties, which is probably why he quickly assumed a sense of seniority.

Arthur Mitchell used to bat with his cap pulled down over the right eye, and the more runs he scored, the further round the cap went, though (according to Cardus) it was not until he had reached 50, 'after two hours or more', that he allowed it to come to rest with the peak over his right ear! Emmott Robinson played with his cap well over the *left* eye, and was what would today be called a 'bowling all-rounder'.

I suppose the Roses matches in the earlier half of this century might have been designed with Emmott Robinson in mind. It is said that he was the first to arrive on one occasion, so he knelt down in the dressing-room and offered up a prayer which went something along these lines: 'Oh Almighty God, thou alone can decide what the weather will be like for this match. If it is fine and Lancashire play better they will win. And if Yorkshire play better, *they* will win. But, oh dear Lord, if thar will just keep out on it for t'next three days, we'll knock bloody 'ell out on 'em.'

Cricket in general and the Lancashire match in particular was always a matter of life or death to Emmott. He lived and breathed the very essence of every game he played in. Even when he was long retired and started to serve as an umpire, he simply could not contain his personal involvement.

At a Test match at Trent Bridge, in 1938, he watched admiringly as Charlie Barnett scored 98 before lunch on the first day, and when play resumed he was standing at square-leg as the final two runs were added to complete Barnett's century. Emmott just could not restrain himself: he raced in and shook the batsman warmly by the hand. It was, I believe, the first and last time Emmott umpired in a Test match.

8

═══

Sir Leonard Hutton

Len Hutton's first-class career, 1934–55, was interrupted by five wartime years, yet he still scored 40,140 runs at an average of 55.51. In his 79 Test matches he scored 6,791 runs (average 56.67), and in 1953 was appointed England's first professional captain, which he celebrated by winning back the Ashes. He then led England in the West Indies to a drawn series, two matches each, and in Australia in 1954–5 his team won the Test series by three matches to one. He subsequently retired from Test cricket and was knighted in 1956.

Len Hutton was, quite simply, the greatest batsman I ever saw. I am not claiming that he was the greatest batsman of all time – I never saw Bradman bat, or Jack Hobbs, or Herbert Sutcliffe, and for obvious reasons I never saw Grace – but Leonard was, without any shadow of a doubt, the greatest batsman I ever saw. I don't use the term 'great' lightly. It should be reserved for those who showed the highest degree of cricketing skills, and is a word which is bandied about too easily and too readily these days. One hears it applied all too often in modern cricket, and that is wrong. 'Great' is a word which should be saved for the very special few who are gifted above all others.

Such a man was Leonard Hutton. I watched him in awe, from long range and, on certain privileged occasions, from rather closer quarters, and let me assure you, he was unbelievable. To begin with, he had the grace of a ballet dancer. His bodyweight seemed always to be perfectly carried and distributed, and he could gauge to perfection just how much he put into a stroke.

Once, while I was batting with him against Gloucestershire, he played a late cut, that most delicate of strokes, and as the ball raced away towards the third-man boundary we could hear the opposition calling to the pursuing fieldsman, 'Let it go for four.' The new ball was almost due and they wanted to use it to get at me, a young man not noted at that time for his batting. For the moment, however, Leonard simply wanted the strike, and as we crossed for the second run he said to me, 'We'll take three . . . it won't go for four.' He knew, you see, just how much weight he had put into the shot. I gulped a bit at that, but Leonard was right. The fieldsman slowed down, giving the ball every chance to reach the ropes, but it pulled up a few feet short. Leonard, having completed the third run, leaned easily on his bat, waiting for the ball to be returned and the new over to start. I regarded him with even greater respect (if it were possible) after that.

My first encounter with Leonard came before the first day of the Roses match at Old Trafford in 1949. Leonard came into the dressing-room wearing his usual garb of a long mackintosh and a trilby, and shook hands with me. 'Freddie Trueman?' he said. 'I'm Len Hutton. I hope you'll have a very successful career.'

That wasn't *quite* our first meeting, in fact. I had bowled at him in the Yorkshire nets as a seventeen-year-old, but I never dreamed the day would come when I would play alongside him in the same Yorkshire team. During that 1949 season he had missed the matches against Cambridge and Oxford Universities, and I had missed the opening three or four county championship matches. Now here we were, on the morning of Saturday, 4 June 1949 . . . my first game with Len Hutton.

After he had changed, Leonard asked me if I would go to the nets and bowl to him for a bit, so off I happily trotted. After a few deliveries of a bit above medium pace, he said, 'Right, now will you take your full run and send me a few more at full pace?'

Leonard scored 201 on the first innings and 91 not out in the second, before Yorkshire's declaration. I didn't take a wicket in the game and I didn't bat, either, but I like to think that little session in the nets might have had some effect upon the game.

There is one detail on the scorecard of that game which I recall with pleasure: 'N. D. Howard, c Trueman b Hutton, 9.' My first championship catch, and it was off one of Leonard's leg-breaks! It seems often to be forgotten that Len was a pretty good bowler of leg-spin, and did a great deal of it, especially in pre-war seasons; he could give the ball quite a tweak.

There was, I suppose, a difference between Leonard's cricket before the war and the stuff he played afterwards . . . except that, to me, he just seemed to get better and better. I remember watching a century against Sussex in 1949 and marvelling at the way he simply took an attack to pieces. I must have been thinking aloud, because Norman Yardley said to me, 'Ah, you should have seen him before the war when he *wanted* to play.'

That was a figure of speech, of course, but there almost certainly was a difference in Len's attitude after the war. It is sometimes forgotten that he sustained an injury to his left wrist while serving in the Army Physical Training Corps, and it was certainly nothing trivial. He spent a total of eighteen months in hospital, undergoing operations and bone grafts from both legs. After all that his left arm ended up shorter than his right, which meant all kinds of adjustments in technique and, even more to the point, a great deal of pain. Very few people knew about this because no one heard Leonard complain. Remember – at Test level, he was now facing Lindwall and Miller, one of the greatest pairs of fast bowlers of all time.

I recall one morning at The Oval in 1951 noticing that Leonard was flexing his left arm and wincing every time he moved it. He was doing it quietly, in a corner, and no one was supposed to notice. Certainly no one said anything about it – except a certain young fast bowler, a new boy. I asked, 'Is it bothering you?'

Len didn't say anything for a minute or two, then admitted, 'Aye, it's giving me some bother every time I pick the bat up.'

It didn't need a genius to work out that an opening batsman playing a big innings would have to 'pick the bat up' quite a lot, and pretty smartly, too. However, Len's solution to his problems was not to pronounce himself unfit to play. Instead, he sent for Joe Parkinson, our 'bat man' – not too many players had personal contracts with manufacturers at that time – who was the linkman with our batmakers in a factory at Horbury. Joe then produced what we called a 'Harrow' bat, the lighter type normally used by schoolboys, even though Leonard normally played with a bat weighing only 2lbs 2ozs, like most of the great batsmen of his day, Bradman included. That day at The Oval, against Surrey, he went out with a schoolboy's bat . . . and scored 151, against the most effective attack in the country, which won seven consecutive county championship titles in the 1950s. Peter Loader had just started playing for Surrey at that time, but they had Alec Bedser and Stuart Surridge to use the new ball, plus Jim Laker, the best off-spinner in the world, and Tony Lock, one of the most effective left-arm spinners this country has produced. A big hundred with a schoolboy's bat – my admiration of the man just grew and grew.

Reg Perks, who opened the bowling for Worcestershire for so many years, told me a lovely little story about his first encounter with Leonard in 1934, when Len would be only seventeen or eighteen. The young man scored 196 and, said Reg, 'We were all mightily impressed. You could see that here was somebody a bit different, a youngster who was clearly going to be a great player.'

When the return game against Worcestershire came round, the opposition were naturally a bit surprised to learn that Hutton was not in the Yorkshire side, and asked where he was.

It so happened that the enquiry was addressed to the most realistic and perhaps most cynical of Yorkshire players, Arthur 'Ticker' Mitchell, who responded without a second's hesitation, 'Oh, him. He's in t'second team getting his feet back on t'ground.' There was very little sentiment around in the Yorkshire ranks of those days.

Perks remarked, 'If he'd been with us, he'd have got a ten-year contract after that innings at Worcester.'

What about Leonard's reputation for being a bit 'tight' where money was concerned? Well, *that* reputation was certainly well deserved. He was a Yorkshireman after all, wasn't he? He once asked me to get him a packet of cigarettes when we were travelling on a train between matches. I didn't argue (no one argued with senior players, not even after the war), and went for the cigarettes. This was the early 1950s, and

they cost three shillings and fourpence (less than twenty pence in modern currency but a fairly sizeable amount at the time, especially to a junior professional), and Leonard 'forgot' to pay me for them.

Being a bit of a Yorkshireman myself, I mentioned this to him from time to time over the years but I didn't get the money . . . until 1988. Yorkshire CCC staged a celebration dinner in Leeds to mark the fiftieth anniversary of Leonard's 364 against Australia at The Oval, and during the evening Leonard handed me an envelope. It contained the equivalent of three and fourpence – all in modern copper coins!

On tour in the West Indies in 1954, a chap approached us to ask if we would like a supply of cigarettes, and the captain (one L. Hutton) gratefully accepted the offer of two hundred for each player. Leonard then counted up the non-smokers in the party – Kenny Suttle, Peter May, Tom Graveney and Alan Moss, while Godfrey Evans and myself were pipe-smokers – and collected *their* allocation for himself. I reckon he saved himself about £400 that time. When cigarettes were being handed around, Leonard never offered his own, and Tony Lock used to remark bitterly that Len brought *his* out of the packet already lit!

It was much the same with drinks. He once invited me to have a drink at Lord's, and I was so shaken I almost forgot to accept. I recovered in time . . . only to see Leonard take the drink out of the MCC cocktail cabinet!

There was one great story – I hope it was a true one – of a very young Hutton getting 50 for Pudsey St Lawrence in a Bradford League game and stopping to listen as the collecting-box went round the ground. He is said to have remarked to his partner, as he cocked an ear, 'That sounded like a *sixpence* going in.'

Len's sense of humour was wry, dry and, quite often, whimsical. I remember once when he was skippering Yorkshire at Headingley against Somerset (Norman Yardley must have been off the field for some reason), he was fielding at mid-off, when I knocked a stump out of the ground. As it went cartwheeling away, he remarked (as much to himself as to me), 'That's one of the greatest sights in cricket.' Then he added, almost as an afterthought, 'It's even better when it's not yours.'

By and large Len preferred to let his bat do the talking for him. The 1951 South Africans included in their party the fast bowler Cuan McCarthy, whose action was, you might say, a little suspect. To English players it was something more than that, and he was usually referred to as 'three-balls-a-tanner'. Before the Yorkshire game at Bramall Lane, McCarthy had been quoted in a newspaper as saying he would 'pin back the ears' of the county's opening pair, Hutton and Frank Lowson. This was the subject of some discussion in the dressing-room, and we waited with more than our usual interest to see what would happen. What happened was that Leonard scored 156 and Frank 115. McCarthy was not quoted on what he thought about that.

Not everything amused Len, by any stretch of imagination. He was not too pleased when, in a Festival game at Scarborough, Trevor Bailey ran in and bowled an apple at him, but he middled it, just the same!

In all the cricket I've played, it may seem a bit odd that one or two shots stick out in the mind, but I certainly recall a six he hit over extra cover against Derbyshire at Park Avenue, Bradford. That was a pitch which more often than not gave a bit of help to the bowler, and Les Jackson and Cliff Gladwin were one of the great pairs in county cricket. I am not sure which of them was bowling at the time, but Leonard's six was one of the greatest shots I have ever seen. It is still absolutely clear in my mind getting on for forty years later.

There was a confidence about Len which had nothing to do with bigheadedness. It seemed that when he was on song he could do no wrong, and when he felt in that mood, nothing was impossible.

At Trent Bridge, again in 1951, I had bowled out Notts fairly cheaply, and Leonard was padding up before starting the Yorkshire innings. First of all he lit a cigarette, as usual – Leonard would never have made a role model for the anti-smoking lobby

– then he said, almost to himself, 'I think I'll make it ninety-six today.'

I happened to be sitting close to him and caught the remark, which struck me as curious. 'Why stop at ninety-six?' I asked. 'Is there something wrong with going for a hundred?'

Len laughed. 'No, I didn't mean *runs*,' he said. 'What I meant was I think I'll make it ninety-six hundreds today.'

And he did. More than that, a few weeks later he completed his hundred hundreds. There were still another twenty-nine to come before he retired in 1955. Perhaps the most important thing to remember about his career was this: he had less than six full seasons of first-class cricket before the war, and he then lost six years of sporting life, from the age of twenty-three to twenty-nine. Who can say what he might have accomplished if it had not been for the loss of those vital years of his youth?

For myself, it is enough that I played *with* him and *under* him as my England captain. At close quarters, I was able to witness batsmanship of a quality I have rarely seen equalled, and never surpassed.

9

Walter Reginald Hammond

Probably the best batsman England has ever produced. A good enough bowler at medium pace to take 732 wickets, and a brilliant fielder who held 819 catches, mostly at slip, he even made three stumpings. He played 405 matches for Gloucestershire and 85 Tests for England with a highest score of 336 not out. Remarkably, he had 36 double centuries and three triples.

Now here really was a giant of a man. I never saw him play but I have talked to many who did – men of the stature of Len Hutton, Denis Compton, Cyril Washbrook, Bill Edrich, Les Ames – and, to a man, they insist that Wally Hammond had a talent that was unique. My dear friend Brian Johnston, with whom I did so much broadcasting, used positively to *glow* at the mere mention, and the memory, of Wally Hammond.

When I first met Hammond during a match at Old Trafford, I was immediately impressed by his physique. He had strong shoulders and a deep chest, and gave the impression of great power. That impression must have been right, because Walter

Hadlee, that fine New Zealand batsman, once told me his hand was broken fielding a shot from Hammond, out on the boundary edge in front of the pavilion.

Hammond must have had particularly fond memories of New Zealand. During the 1932–3 tour, as the number three batsman he saw Herbert Sutcliffe dismissed off the first ball of the innings, and had scarcely got off the mark himself before Sutcliffe's opening partner, Eddie Paynter, was bowled. A duck for each of the openers and Hammond then scored 227! He didn't hang about, either, because his fifth-wicket partnership with Ames put on 242 in 144 minutes. In the following game, in Auckland, he made 336 in 318 minutes (in fact his third hundred took only 47 minutes), and his average at the end of the two-match rubber was 563.

Oh yes, I would dearly have loved to see him play and, better still, to have bowled at him. This is not intended in any way to be an immodest desire; good bowlers have always enjoyed operating against great batsmen, because it is as much a mental as a physical exercise. I learned that, sometimes the hard way, bowling to the three West Indian Ws and against Gary Sobers, plus, of course, some of the great Australian players.

Hammond was a generation ahead of me, however. He headed the first-class batting averages in England for eight successive seasons, 1933–46, and was yet another of those players who lost six years of his playing life to the war. Who knows what he might have achieved? One wonders what else there was for him to achieve, though.

Hammond must have been the outstanding close-catcher of the 1930s – people I know remember that on catches alone he made newspaper headlines. He took ten for Gloucestershire against Surrey and scored a century in each innings as well.

Hammond had a best bowling performance of 9 for 23 to his credit, and he must, I suppose, have regarded it as a disappointment that he never took all ten in an innings. There wasn't much else for him to achieve. On top of all this, he played association football for Bristol Rovers, was a scratch golfer and an expert and enthusiastic bridge player.

After our first, almost casual, meeting at Old Trafford I began to read a lot about his career and his records, and I talked to as many people as I could find who had competed against him. They all said the same thing: Walter Reginald Hammond was something very special indeed.

I was, quite frankly, absolutely fascinated by what I had read and heard about him. For instance, George Emmett, the opening batsman for Gloucestershire before and after the war, had told me how he used to get 'fed up' with batting after Wally had come in, because he rarely had a chance to face a ball, such was Hammond's appetite for the strike. There have been quite a few batsmen who have pinched the strike when the pitch was good and the bowling not too difficult, but nothing like the number who have positively demanded the strike in every innings.

'That's just how it was with Hammond,' said Emmett, mournfully. 'I remember once against Glamorgan I was on fifty when our first wicket fell and Wally came in. After tea, I was now in the sixties but he was way past a hundred and showed no signs of letting up or giving me a piece of the bowling. He was absolutely insatiable when he was in *that* mood. I was utterly fed up and thought I might just as well get back to the dressing-room and sit down to watch it.'

Len Hutton had a different story to tell. 'I *hated* batting with him,' he said of Hammond, 'because it was his idea of a joke to hit the ball back at his partner, and he hit it so hard that you had to be constantly wide awake if you wanted to avoid injury. He once drove one back which I couldn't avoid, so I turned my back on the shot – and it felt as though someone had stuck a knife between my shoulder-blades.'

Peter West, the radio and TV commentator, had yet another view of Hammond to recount. 'Hammond was in the middle of a hand of bridge when he was called upon to go out to bat. He laid the cards, face down, on the table and warned the other

three, "Don't anyone touch those cards until I return." He went out, scored a fast hundred and came back to finish the game.'
A modern Francis Drake?

Harold Larwood remembers a game for Notts against Gloucestershire at Bristol. 'We had about forty minutes to bowl at them towards the end of the day. One wicket fell and in came Hammond. It was the sort of situation which demanded a bit of care in the final few minutes of the day, and when a nightwatchman is usually sent in. Not with Hammond around. He strode out to the middle, started to score runs, and when I bowled the last ball of the day, he hit it on to the roof of the pavilion for six.'

I was aware that after the war Hammond had gone to live in South Africa, and so it was that when I went there on an International Cavaliers tour in 1960 I resolved to look him up. I wanted to see more of this man and to talk to him. Thus, in Durban with the Cavaliers, I made enquiries about where he lived.

To the great regret of the South Africans, Hammond took no interest in first-class cricket once he had settled there, and was never seen on any of the grounds. Nevertheless, it was not difficult to find out where he lived.

That evening, at close of play, my mate Brian Statham asked, 'What are we doing tonight?'

I answered, 'I'll tell you what *I* am doing – I'm going to see Wally Hammond.'

Brian immediately said, 'Then I'm coming, too.'

So did Geoff Pullar. Then our manager, the much-loved journalist Ron Roberts, chipped in, 'I'd like to come as well.'

We piled into a taxi and drove out to Hammond's home in the suburbs. I knocked at the door and said to the lady who opened it, 'I'm Freddie Trueman and I'd like to see Mr Hammond if that is possible. I've got some friends with me . . .'

A voice inside the house called, 'Bring 'em in.'

Well, he might have been out of sorts with cricket – I didn't know why and I didn't ask – but he was a splendid host. He had his own bar in one room, and that was soon opened, and we talked cricket until the early hours. No one wanted to leave, including the manager of the tour.

I remember Wally saying he couldn't understand why wickets were being covered in England. 'We produce the best cricketers in the world in all playing conditions,' he said, 'because pitches are uncovered, and we are robbing ourselves of the one great advantage we have over other countries.' That is something which holds true to this day and Hammond's view was absolutely right.

It was a marvellous evening of cricket talk, and as we left I pleaded with him to agree to come to the game the following day. I sent a car for him – and he came. I have always been very glad about that. I told him we all hoped to see him again, at cricket in England, but we never did because he passed away in 1965. What a man! What a player he must have been!

One final memory of him, from Norman Yardley, who was in the party when Hammond captained England for the last time, on tour in 1946–7: 'Wally loved to drive. No distance seemed too great for him if he got behind the wheel of a car. One evening he roped in a couple of us and we drove a round trip of 180 miles to attend a dinner party. Naturally it was very late when we got back to our hotel and I, for one, slept very late. When I got up I found that Hammond had beaten me to it by a long way. He had scored over two hundred.'

10

Raymond Russell Lindwall and Keith Ross Miller

Lindwall, one of the great fast bowlers of all time, was my idol and my hero. Fifty matches for New South Wales were followed by 34 for Queensland after he had made his home in Brisbane. Seventeen years old when the Second World War broke out, he was another of the players who 'lost' six vital years of his youth. Yet he still managed to take 228 wickets in 61 Tests. Miller, one of the the most accomplished all-rounders of post-war years, averaged nearly 37 runs and took 170 wickets in his 55 Tests.

June 1952, and the First Test against India at Headingley – my first Test as well. As if that were not thrill enough for any youngster, I was sitting in the dressing-room during a tea interval when a man walked in wearing a raincoat over his grey suit, and highly polished black shoes. His arrival was greeted with warmth, though a touch of surprise, by players like Len Hutton, Denis Compton and Godfrey Evans. They all responded cordially: 'Hello, Ray. How are you? What brings you here?'

I thought to myself, this must be the man. This was the man I admired above all fast bowlers I have ever seen. I recall that beautiful accelerating approach to the wicket and the magnificently controlled outswing. He was cricket's answer to Louis Armstrong – the King of Swing. I have always been convinced that if Beethoven had lived 150 years later than he did, he would have written a symphony as the only adequate way of describing Lindwall's bowling. I was twenty-one years old; Ray would have been thirty, and four years earlier he had toured England with Bradman's Australians and taken 86 wickets at 15.68. Figures apart, though, it was the sheer majesty of his bowling which had captured my imagination.

Now, in 1952, he was back in England as a professional in the Lancashire League, and I remember reading that his pace was just a bit too much for the slip fieldsmen when his outswinger found the edge at ninety miles an hour. He had been forced to develop an inswinger to claim some of the wickets his pace merited. And here he was in the same room as me. This was something else to tell my dad, whose eyes used to mist over when I went home and told him about some of the great names I was now meeting.

Ray chatted for some moments to the senior players in the dressing-room, then walked over to me. 'Freddie Trueman? Hello, I'm Ray Lindwall,' he said. And a friendship was born, although I didn't realise it at the time. As far as I was concerned, I was in the presence of a god.

To my amazement, Ray sat down alongside me and, with disarming frankness, told me he had been asked to come along and have a look at me by the Australian Board of Control. Apparently, there had been some talk about me, and as the Aussies were due to tour in 1953 they thought it might be as well to have an expert view of this young man.

Having said that, Lindwall then began to talk cricket to me in a modest and unassuming way. 'You have a good approach,' he said, 'but try to slow the start down a little bit and *flow* into

it, accelerating in the last four or five paces. Then you'll find
you can get a bit more pace. And try to shorten your delivery
stride, just a little bit.'

Here was the king of them all telling me this – the man who had
been asked to report on me to the Australian Board of Control.
I could scarcely believe what I was hearing. As far as I was
concerned, it was privilege enough that he had come across to
talk to me at all. The advice was a very considerable bonus.

It was in later years that Ray and I became close personal
friends and exchanged many confidences. He told me, for
instance, that as a boy, his idol was a spin bowler, although
he never wavered in his own intention to bowl fast. He must
have lived somewhere near Bill O'Reilly in Sydney at that time,
because he used to see him around in the streets. Enjoying a
schoolboy game, as soon as he saw O'Reilly he would let one
go as fast as he could and look up expectantly: 'How was that,
Mr O'Reilly?'

When the 1953 tourists arrived I didn't get into the England
side until the final Test at The Oval. The previous four had been
drawn, and when we at last won, it brought back the Ashes
after a record absence of nearly nineteen years. What a thrill
that was for the young Trueman. Not only that, but Lindwall
was Australia's top scorer (with 62) in the first innings until he
was last out, c Evans b Trueman. Laker and Lock wrapped it up
for us in the second innings, but there was no happier cricketer
in England at that moment than F. S. Trueman. However, it
was during that match that Ray bowled a short-pitched ball
– not a full bouncer, but one which *did* bounce – and hit me
around the shoulder joint. It really did hurt, but I didn't say
anything.

Five and a half years later, during the 1958–9 England
tour to Australia, Ray had moved from New South Wales
to Queensland, and when we reached Brisbane he greeted
me with: 'Come and have a beer.' (I should mention that he
absolutely loved beer. He didn't just drink it – he devoured it.)
Now that, of course, was the 'chucking' tour, with Meckiff,

Rorke and Slater all picked ahead of the great Lindwall, and he was bitterly disappointed. He might have been in his late thirties but he still believed he could do a job of work at Test level, and do it legally.

With Australia two up in the series he was recalled for the Fourth and Fifth Tests, and in Melbourne he had the distinction of getting Trevor Bailey out for a 'pair'. When Ray came in to bat, I let him have a bouncer which he fended off his face and was caught by Colin Cowdrey.

With that choice Australian term of endearment, Ray said, 'You little bastard – what did you do that for?'

I replied, 'What's the matter? I didn't say anything when you hit me at The Oval in 1953.'

He gazed at me in astonishment. 'Do you remember that?' he asked.

'I certainly do,' I told him.

'Right,' said Lindwall, 'I'll see you at half past six for a drink.'

Some years later we were together in South Africa for their centenary celebrations and we spent every spare minute together. It was then that I learned for the first time that Lindwall was a devout Christian and would not miss going to church on Sunday.

During that time in South Africa we often swopped notes on the way we gripped the ball. Ray held it with two fingers apart and the seam between them; I controlled it by using two fingers close together to grip the seam. I found it fascinating that we both made the ball leave the bat but with a different grip. That was the one, he said, that got the *good* players out.

Ray had tremendous respect for Len Hutton, whom he considered one of the finest batsmen he had ever bowled against, and for Denis Compton as a magnificent entertainer of a batsman. He was also a great admirer of Alec Bedser, and I think one of the great disappointments of his life was not to have beaten Alec's record of 236 Test wickets. Ray even went to India (something not too many fast bowlers of

that era risked!) to try to overtake Alec, and had to be flown home, seriously ill.

We talked about the inswinger, which he had found necessary to develop in the Lancashire League. He said that dropping the left shoulder a little earlier opened him up a bit, and he found he could make the ball go back in to the batsman. I went off to the nets and tried it and, sure enough, it worked. It gave me another string to my bow, and I couldn't believe how easy it was to do.

Much as I admired him as a bowler, my personal friendship with Ray became equally important to me. As soon as I got to Brisbane I rang his number and heard that familiar voice respond, 'Lindwall the Florists,' and off we'd go for a drink and a natter, or perhaps a round of golf. He was a fine player. His mates always called him 'Killer', but I gave him his full title, in that pedantic Yorkshire way, of 'Raymond Russell'.

In his later years he had some problems, and I got a phone call from Australia to ask if I would fly out to speak at a couple of dinners for him. There was no argument about that. 'Of course I will,' I replied, and I'm glad to say that at the end of that fund-raising effort we had raised, I think, $68,000.

He will always remain, to me, the greatest fast bowler I ever saw. He will also remain one of the nicest people I have ever met – I never heard him say a wrong thing about anybody.

Ray's great bowling partner was, of course, Keith Miller, and that partnership will always be remembered as one of the greatest of all time. Miller was a superb athlete with an immense personality. A handsome man, and wartime pilot, he was a bowler who could be frighteningly fast, but who was quite capable of slinging down a leg-break at you as well. He could bowl anything. I was never as closely involved with Keith in a personal way as I was with Lindwall, but I had immense respect for him.

Keith was, of course, a close friend of Denis Compton, which is not surprising since they were similar personalities, and there are a thousand stories about him . . .

Can you imagine his captain, Bradman, steely and stern, coming down to breakfast in a London hotel and meeting, on the stairs, K. R. Miller, resplendent in black tie and dinner jacket, just returning from a night out? Or Miller, as captain of New South Wales, leading his team on to the field before someone pointed out he had *eleven* followers. What does Miller do but position his key fieldsmen, the close-catchers, before addressing the remainder: 'And one of you lot – bugger off back to the dressing-room . . . I don't care which one.'

I once recorded a radio programme with Keith, and I was talking about the time I got him out twice in the Lord's Test of 1956 when he interrupted, with a laugh, 'Just hang on a minute. Do you remember, in 1953, Australians versus Combined Services—'

It was my turn to interrupt. 'Yes, I do remember,' I said. 'You got 250 or 260 not out against me.'

Lindwall and Miller . . . what a pair! They were, I think, opposites in terms of personality and approach to life, but put them together on a cricket field with a ball in their hands – and look out!

In 1980, when the centenary of Tests between England and Australia brought so many fine players to this country, Ray Lindwall (with another marvellous Aussie, Neil Harvey) came up to my home for an evening. Ray looked out at the view over the garden to the green hills of the Yorkshire Dales, put his arm around my shoulders and said, 'FS, it's wonderful. And it's no more or less than you deserve.'

Last year I was in one of the hospitality boxes at Lord's and I nearly cried when I saw Keith Miller, this magnificent athlete, walking with the help of a Zimmer frame. We sat and chatted about many things, but most of all about Lindwall. After that meeting, I said goodbye to him before his flight home. Keith felt it would be his last trip to England. I hoped not, but feared that it might well be.

Veronica and I spent that night with friends in Essex, and the following day we were driving home up the M11, when somewhere round about Cambridge I heard on the car radio that Ray Lindwall had passed away. I had to stop the car. A great big lump developed in my throat as I thought of Ray and of how much we had shared. Then I remembered Keith Miller, who had also shared so much with him. He would hear the news as he flew home to Australia.

The BBC telephoned me at home for a tribute to the great man. With infinite sadness, I said, 'The king is dead.'

11

===

Arthur Brian Sellers

Brian Sellers played in 334 matches for Yorkshire between 1932 and 1948 and was captain for almost all of them. The son of an opening batsman of the 1890s, Sellers rigidly adhered to the cherished traditions of the county while insisting on the Yorkshireman's God-given right to call a spade a bloody shovel. He was blunt, uncompromising, tough and forthright. While not a gifted player himself, he led Yorkshire to county championships in 1933, 1935, 1937, 1938, 1939 and 1946. He afterwards served on the county committee until 1972, for most of that time as cricket chairman.

When, as a youngster of eighteen, I joined the Yorkshire first team, Johnny Wardle gave me this advice: 'There's only one fellow you have to look out for round here. His name is Sellers. Nobody else matters.'

How right he was. Brian Sellers was one on his own. He had made his first appearance for Yorkshire at Lord's long before the war, and as an amateur in a team of professionals, he had his own dressing-room and emerged from the pavilion on to the field through a separate gate. Although he was the captain of the side, he made the mistake of not going to see his men before the start of that game. As the time for play to start approached and no captain appeared to address his troops, those grizzled veterans of many a championship encounter looked at each other and muttered darkly.

When Sellers was seen, through the dressing-room window, to walk through the amateurs' gate and on to the field, Herbert Sutcliffe, the senior pro – and very much a believer in doing things in a proper manner – halted the professionals as they prepared to follow the captain: 'Wait just a minute or two.' And they allowed Sellers to walk right to the middle and stand, for a moment, on his own. He must have felt the loneliest man in the world: Lord's, on a Saturday in high summer . . . the ground full . . . a captain on parade, but no team. It was only then that Sutcliffe said, 'Right. Let's get out there.'

Telling this story, years later, Herbert reflected, 'To be fair to the man, he never did it again.' Sellers never referred to that experience but I am pretty sure he never forgot it – it must have affected his thinking and his attitude in the years that followed.

It is always held in Yorkshire that if there are ten *other* good players in a side, it doesn't matter who is the captain. It's an over-simplification, I know – good captains can have a profound influence on the way a game takes shape – but there is no doubt that in the thirties, Sellers had a very good side indeed with him. Even so, there were times when things went wrong . . .

At Huddersfield, in 1935, Yorkshire batted first and were bowled out for 31 by Essex – a despised team of no-hopers as far as Yorkshire were concerned – and lost by an innings in a season in which they won the championship.

The story goes that a member arrived just a bit late, saw a scoreboard which read 29 for 9, and asked, 'Who's done the damage – Bowes?'

The answer he was given was: 'No – he's batting!'

Nevertheless, Yorkshire in the 1930s were undoubtedly a

great side. According to old players I have talked to, Sellers, in his early days, would occasionally come out with, 'My father says . . .'

One day an exasperated George Macaulay told him, 'Here's t'ball, then. Get your dad to come and ball these bastards out.' I think Sellers must have got a good deal of his basic philosophy from Macaulay.

I had some monumental clashes with Sellers because, as chairman, he ran the club, and especially the first team, like a medieval warlord. He would curse and swear like a trooper, and you could believe, if you were terribly misguided, that he was 'one of the boys'. However, he was the first to demand total and absolute respect for the elder statesmen of the club.

In fact I didn't have to wait too long in my Yorkshire career before we had our first 'barney'. In 1952, I took 8 for 31 against India at Old Trafford. I knew that Len Hutton was going to ask the Indians to follow on, and as I was perspiring profusely, I wanted to have a quick shower and change my shirt. I made the mistake of walking quickly but quietly off the field as soon as possible.

It was weeks later, during the Roses match, that I paid a visit to the toilet and Sellers followed me.

'I've been wantin' to have a word with thee,' he stormed. 'Just who the hell do you think you are, walking off the field first at Old Trafford?'

I had to think for a minute to understand what he was talking about – much had happened since the Third Test. Then I realised what it was and explained that I had hurried off to change my shirt.

'I don't give a bugger about that,' said the chairman. 'In future, wait until you are *asked* to go off the field first.'

Mind you, he didn't always have the last word. I remember skippering Yorkshire against Pakistan, and Sellers handed me the names of the team which the committee had selected. Duggie Padgett's name was not on the list so I told the chairman I was including Duggie.

'No, you're not,' he said.

'Yes, I am,' I retorted in a heated conversation which sounded like something out of a pantomime. 'And I'll tell you something else – Sharpe is going to open the batting. *That's* not on your list.'

'He's bloody well not opening,' said Sellers.

'He bloody well is,' I insisted, and off we went again.

Of course, once the game was ready to begin, I took over as captain and what happened after that had nothing to do with the committee. Padgett played, Sharpe opened (and scored 197) and I waited to see what Sellers would have to say about that.

At the end of the game he simply said, quietly, 'Well done. There'll be a pint waiting for you when you've changed.'

That was ABS, the Crackerjack, as he was known to pre-war players, all over. He would deliver a rocket where he thought one was justified and then never refer to the incident again. He liked to get the unpleasantness out of the way and say, 'Reight. Now let's go and have a pint.' He never bore a grudge, and he tried, in his own way, to be fair. It just didn't always work out like that . . .

In 1963, I was summoned to appear before the committee in late June, and I arrived not knowing what to expect. As I stood before them in all their magisterial glory, I was told that a letter of complaint had been received from a hotel in Bristol. During Yorkshire's game against Gloucestershire, I was told, there had been a lot of noise, singing and games, which had disturbed other residents, and I, as captain, was being held responsible.

'Just a minute,' I protested. 'While the game at Bristol was going on I was playing for England against the West Indies at Lord's. It was quite a remarkable Test match and got a lot of publicity in the papers. Brian Close got seventy, which largely saved the game. Colin Cowdrey went in at the end with a broken forearm to help England make a draw. Oh yes, and I got eleven wickets in the match. I thought you might have noticed.'

Jimmy Binks had actually been the captain in Bristol, but I never heard that *he* had been called before the committee and given a bollocking.

I have always been a proud Yorkshireman and, like so many other boys of my day, I thought it was absolutely tremendous to be promoted through various stages to become a county bowler. My disillusionment with Yorkshire CCC was by no means a sudden thing. It was something which happened gradually, over a long period of time and a choking series of snubs, rebuffs and disappointments.

In March 1963, in Christchurch, New Zealand, I overtook my mate Brian Statham's world record of 242 Test wickets, and during that match I reached a total of 250. The New Zealand Board of Control, in a gesture which I have never forgotten, had the ball mounted and inscribed, and at the dinner which followed the match, they presented it to me. The following day the telegrams of congratulations began to arrive . . . from friends and ordinary supporters of the game, from sixteen county clubs, even one from the MCC. But from Yorkshire – nothing!

When I took my 300th Test wicket, and people said it would never be done again – little knowing that in a few years' time Tests would be played all the year round – I retrieved the ball from the umpires' room and had it mounted myself.

Yorkshire decided something *ought* to be done and authorised me to spend 'up to a hundred guineas' on a suitable memento. It then cost me as much again of my own money to buy a tea service to go with the club's silver tray. When it came to the presentation I remember Sir William Worsley, the president, saying, 'What's this? It doesn't seem very much for such a feat.' What do you think he was told? John Nash, the secretary, told Sir William, 'He's lucky to get that. Thieves broke into the office during the winter and took everything except the tray!'

When we won the county championship in 1959 (after what had been the longest interval in the modern history of the club) our reward was a cheque for fifty pounds. A certain amount of telephoning went on between the players because we felt we ought to show our contempt by not saying 'thank you' to the committee.

This – inevitably, I suppose – reached the ears of the chairman, who tackled me about it. Sellers had a firm belief that everyone was guilty until he had proved himself innocent. I had played no part in starting the rumbles of discontent, but that didn't stop Sellers telling me, 'I knew *you* would have something to say about it.'

Then came the matter of the beard ... An electric shaver company offered me a thousand pounds to grow a beard, so that in due course they could feature it being shaved off in an advertisement. I arrived at Bramall Lane for the Roses match with the beginnings of a fairly healthy hirsute appendage.

The chairman went mad: 'You can get that lot shaved off straightaway,' he roared. I mildly pointed out that the shaver firm were paying me more to grow it than Yorkshire paid me for a year's service, but that cut no ice with the Crackerjack. 'You haven't asked permission to grow a beard, so get it off. We want no seafaring buggers in here.' I fulfilled my contract with the firm.

Yes, there was something quite magnificently feudal about Brian Sellers: he was the warlord and the players were his mercenaries, to be treated as such. However, he didn't like anyone else behaving with similar autocracy. When Herbert Sutcliffe once complained about colourful language in the dressing-room, Sellers told him in no uncertain manner, 'That's *their* territory, and if you don't like the way they talk, keep out.'

I do believe that in his own way, he tried to be fair, and he almost certainly *believed* he was fair. If he was proved wrong, he was never too big to apologise. I am bound to say he rarely thought that he was wrong, but he would, if it became clear to him, admit it.

Above all else in life, I feel sure, Sellers loved Yorkshire cricket, with a passion which made him, at times, blind to many faults. His devotion to the club was complete and absolute.

Yorkshire County Cricket Club, to ABS, was something above and beyond petty grudges and grievances. He loved its traditions, its history, its pre-eminence, and he defended them all with blind, all-consuming dedication.

He once confessed to me that sacking Brian Close and replacing him as captain with Geoffrey Boycott was the worst decision of his life. He died in 1981 of – I am convinced – a broken heart.

12

===

John Arlott,
Brian Johnston and
Test Match Special

It was the summer of 1974 when I joined *Test Match Special* for the first time, along with Don Mosey. Don was a BBC staff producer and an experienced broadcaster who had already sat with the *TMS* team for some years as a producer in the north of England for the Test matches at Headingley and Old Trafford, so he was well acquainted with the team.

I, on the other hand, had done a little bit of braodcasting, usually with Don, an old friend, but the *TMS* commentary box was something different. The operation and technique were completely new to me and brought me into contact with a couple of legendary broadcasters, John Arlott and Brian Johnston. They were absolute giants of their profession, but, more than that, they were fascinating personalities and entirely contrasting types. I came to love them both, and, though nothing could quite equal the personal thrill of being a Yorkshire and England fast bowler, broadcasting brought an extra dimension to my cricketing life and has given me immense pleasure for well over twenty years.

I first remember meeting John Arlott when I was quite a young player. He asked me to join him in a charity match he had arranged, before which we were invited to lunch at his home in Alresford, Hampshire. And what a lunch! It started with shellfish – prawns and mussels, as I recall – and to follow, John had somehow managed to get a whole lobster for each of us. Many of his friends from the Hampshire side were there – Leo Harrison, Peter Sainsbury, Derek Shackleton amongst them – but John took me on one side and said, 'There is someone here I would like you to meet.' And with that, he introduced me to Percy Chapman. Now here was one of the great men of cricket in the 1920s and 1930s . . . A. P. F. Chapman, the man who in 1924 won his first England cap despite the fact that he had played only for Berkshire, a 'minor' county.

I spent a large part of the day talking to this legend of the past. I was delighted to find that Chapman had a strong affection for Maurice Leyland, though I was later to find that this was common all over the world, wherever Maurice had played. Everyone liked him. Most of all, however, I was delighted that Chapman, like so many of his generation, loved his cricket with a passionate intensity and was delighted to reminisce about games, and players, of previous eras.

Lunch that day had given me my first insight into the way John Arlott loved the good things of life, notably food and wine. Little did I realise that I would later spend years sitting beside him in a commentary box.

There was little doubt that John had not enjoyed his earlier days as a policeman in Hampshire. He didn't like the life very much at all, though, as a born raconteur, he remembered many of the most amusing episodes and was happy to retell them. He had the heart and mind of a poet – he was a great admirer and, indeed, friend of Dylan Thomas – and loved to hear that rich voice of Richard Burton reading Thomas's work. John's Hampshire burr gave him an exceptional broadcasting presence, but his real genius lay in finding just the right words to describe any sort of scene or situation. He gave me this advice: 'Sit back, close your eyes and imagine you are describing something to a blind man.' There is no doubt about it: if we wanted something describing to perfection on *Test Match Special*, John was the man to do it.

I remember during that first game we worked together, Pakistan had a bowler called Asif Masood with a strange approach to the wicket. He started his run-in, stopped, reversed, then started again at a different angle. He intrigued us all in different ways. Don Mosey, waiting for his first ever international cricket broadcast, following immediately after Arlott's twenty-minute spell, was racking his brains for a suitable way of describing this run-in of Asif's.

It was then that we heard John solemnly intoning, 'And Asif starts, stops, starts again . . . in the manner of a butler who has opened the doors of the withdrawing-room, been embarrassed by what he has seen, and discreetly withdrawn . . .'

That was it – *exactly* – but expressed in a way that no one else in the box would ever have dreamed of. That was the genius of John Arlott.

John even talked of his own art of description in a poetic way. As he told it to me: 'There are people driving their motorcars, farmers in their fields, shepherds tending their flocks . . . none of them can see what you are seeing. Paint a picture for them. *Make* them visualise it. Bring it to life for them.'

John had gone to South Africa in the late 1940s, and returned loving their wines and hating the system of apartheid in just about equal proportions. He was, of course, an internationally renowned authority on some wines, and was proud of the fact that he had been the *Guardian* newspaper's specialist writer on two subjects: cricket and wine. 'Cardus wasn't the *only* man to write on two specialist subjects,' he once told me.

He used to carry around a briefcase which obviously weighed rather a lot, and in my early days in the commentary box I was naive enough to believe it must hold a portable typewriter, or something like that. I was amazed, then, when I saw him, for the first time, open the briefcase, take out a bottle of red wine and proceed to open it – without pausing in his description of the cricket taking place out in the middle.

Occasionally, John frightened me to death . . . as on the occasion at Lord's when we were due to provide the lunchtime summary together. The system at that time was that the commentator (John) would put a point to the summariser (me), then follow up with as many other questions and answers as were required to fill the five-minute period. The last ball of the morning was bowled, John asked me a question and away I went. When I felt I had said all there was to be said on that point, I mentally prepared myself for the next question and risked a sideways glance to see if John was ready to ask it. To my stark horror, I saw he had slumped forward on to the table and, as far as I could see, was unconscious. I was fast running out of things to say and my partner appeared to have passed out completely! I looked wildly round for help. (The most terrifying sight on earth is a microphone into which you have nothing further to say when a 'live' broadcast is taking place.) It was Don who came to the rescue by slipping into one of the vacant seats and throwing me a verbal lifeline in the form of another question.

The summary over, I looked down at the apparently unconscious John and asked, hoarsely, 'Is he all right? Or is he dead?' At this, John roused himself, stood up and wandered amiably out of the box.

A few minutes later Brian Johnston returned from lunch and was told what had happened. Concerned, he went to our telephone and made a call to the press box. He spoke to John Woodcock, at that time cricket correspondent of *The Times*, and asked if John was there.

'He's sitting opposite me, enjoying a glass of claret,' replied John. So all, it seemed, was well – but you could have fooled me.

John would have loved to play first-class cricket for Hampshire. He did play for the Second XI, and I believe he was once twelfth man for the senior side. He told me he had to go on the field when someone came off, and very soon he was called upon to chase a ball to the boundary, near the members' seats in front of the pavilion.

'I decided,' said John, 'on a Learie Constantine-like back flip of the ball before it crossed the boundary, and I timed this to perfection. I then went on to turn a somersault before getting to my feet to return the ball to the wicket-keeper. I rose, gripping the ball, drew back my arm for the throw . . . and was amazed to see the massed ranks of Worcestershire members parting before me like the Red Sea before the Children of Israel. I was facing the wrong way! I resolved in that moment never to try to emulate Learie Constantine again.'

After writing his book *Fred – Portrait of a Fast Bowler*, John invited me to his home in Alresford to go through the proofs. I was amazed at the stuff I had to ask him to take out: according to John's book Yorkshire almost decided to release me in my early days with the county, which wasn't true. He also said that

I had worn lurid clothing, including a tie with the figure of a naked woman on it – I have never in my life worn such a tie. There were things which I was reported to have said, at home and abroad – things which I had never at any time said. I really was staggered by some of it. John readily agreed to delete the passages I objected to, however, and the result was a book of which he was very proud.

The loss of John to the *TMS* commentary team was an enormous blow. He retired in 1980 after the England v Australia Centenary Test, in a highly emotional moment at Lord's which will be remembered by everybody present. As he completed his final twenty-minute stint at the microphone (without a touch of sentiment or any formal goodbye to radio listeners), the whole crowd stood to pay a massive tribute in which the players on the field joined. If John showed no trace of sentiment, the rest of us in the commentary box made no secret of our feelings.

John firmly believed that the greatest bowler of all time – fast, slow or medium pace – was Sydney Barnes, the legendary 'SF' who was plucked from obscurity in Staffordshire to tour Australia and South Africa with the MCC.

Barnes was a prickly, taciturn character, completely unsuited to the camaraderie of first-class cricket, but was a bowler of mar-vellous versatility. Even *Who's Who* had difficulty in describing him adequately: 'right-arm fast-medium to slow-medium'. The secret, I can well believe, lay in his hands. They were huge, with great long fingers which could work all kinds of magic on the ball. On the only occasion I was introduced to him, I remember my right hand completely disappeared in his clasp.

John had personal experience of the man's genius, which must have been when John was playing for Hampshire Second XI against Staffs, because, apparently, rain stopped play and he and a group of friends persuaded Barnes to carry out a demonstration in the nets whilst the ground was drying out. Now this wasn't easy, as Barnes was not going to reveal any of his secrets easily. He must have been supremely confident in his ability, though, because he allowed himself to be 'persuaded' when money was offered. All his life (and he lived to the age of ninety-four) the old boy believed that the labourer was worthy of his hire – when he was ninety-one, the *Daily Mail* asked to interview him, and he asked, 'How much?'

When John asked Barnes to demonstrate, first, his off-cutter, he said, 'It'll cost you a quid.' This, remember, was long before the war, and no one had a lot of money to throw about. John and his mates clubbed together, however, raised one pound, and Barnes, without any further preparation, bowled a ball at brisk medium-pace which pitched on the off-stump and took the leg-stump. QED. Next, the audience asked for a leg-cutter, and another whipround was necessary before this was shown.

Now let's get something straight before we go any further with this story. The term 'cutter' is much misused, especially by modern TV commentators who, significantly, are almost exclusively former players of recent vintage. The description 'leg-cutter' in particular seems to be applied to any ball which hits the seam and veers from on to off, and nine times out of ten – no, ninety-nine times out of a hundred – it is not a leg-cutter at all.

In New Zealand, in the early part of 1997, a delivery from Heath Davis which bounced a bit during an England innings in Christchurch, was described, quite ludicrously, as 'a steepling leg-cutter bowled at ninety miles an hour', as daft a claim as I have ever heard in my life: a ninety mph leg-cutter! That would be the old original unplayable ball of all time. Remember, if you will (it's been shown enough times on television), the delivery from Shane Warne to Mike Gatting on the first occasion they faced each other, then multiply the speed of the delivery five or six times, and you have, approximately, a 'ninety mph leg-cutter'. Anyone who could bowl that sort of ball, at will, would reasonably have expected to take six wickets an over against a team of Don Bradmans!

A leg-cutter requires the fingers to whip across the seam in a cutting motion, causing the ball, when it pitches, to deviate from on- to off-side. Alec Bedser bowled it beautifully, but I can't think of many other people who could.

So here were John Arlott and his pals, having scraped together another quid, watching as Sydney Francis Barnes pitched a medium-fast delivery, exactly on length, on the line of the leg-stump, which took the off-stump! They would, John told me, have dearly liked to see him remove the remaining stump, but they couldn't raise another pound – so Barnes did it anyway, and took out the middle stump, as clean as a whistle. Perhaps he felt generous in his old age, although I doubt it from what I have heard of the man.

What a bowler he must have been, and how I would have liked to see him in action, and perhaps learned a thing or two from him.

Back to *Test Match Special*, however. From 1974 onwards we settled into a regular format, with John Arlott and Brian Johnston as the regular commentators and Chris Martin-Jenkins, Henry Blofeld and Don Mosey alternating on a perm-two-from-three basis. Trevor Bailey and I were the regular summarisers, and we were occasionally joined by a former overseas Test player, usually when England were at home to India or Pakistan.

We were a team in the very best sense of the word. We incorporated a blend of voices, accents and styles which in the mid-seventies very quickly established *TMS* as highly popular cult broadcasting. It was at this time that we used to 'talk cricket' whenever rain stopped play (or there was a break for any other reasons). We received scores and scores of letters saying, 'We like it best of all when no cricket is being played and you just talk amongst yourselves.' This was something that our television colleagues simply could not understand, any more than they appreciated hearing of the number of people who *watched* TV while *listening* to radio commentary. A large number of people wrote regularly to tell us they did just that, all the same.

We all of us, to a man, thoroughly enjoyed *TMS*, and I think our sense of pleasure communicated itself to the listeners. That's how it seemed, anyway, from the correspondence which came in, and we did get a huge number of letters.

Of these, more were addressed to Brian Johnston than anyone else. Brian was a born communicator. When I first met him I immediately thought of him as sixty-two, going on sixteen. He had just never grown out of his schooldays. He trotted out schoolboy jokes, played schoolboy japes on all of us, talked in schoolboy terminology.

If Brian hadn't been a broadcaster, at which he was an absolute natural, he would, I'm sure, have loved to be on the stage. He seemed to achieve an immediate rapport with his audience, whether he was working in radio or to a packed theatre, where I 'performed' with him many times. His sense of fun, of sheer enjoyment, hit a responsive note right from the start. His puns – so many of them – were excruciating; his gaffes, which he trotted out with wide-eyed (and straight-faced) innocence were absolutely outrageous. Yet he got away with all of them. Who else, for instance, could have come out with 'Illingworth has relieved himself at the Pavilion End,' 'Cowdrey is round the corner, waiting for a tickle between the short legs,' and 'the bowler's Holding, the batsman's Willey'? Only Brian. Never a complaint . . . never an indignant telephone call . . . never an unpleasant letter.

Once he received a letter from a lady which he deemed inadvisable to be read over the airwaves. It came after a streaker had been led away by a policeman who diplomatically placed his helmet over the streaker's most treasured possessions. With an innocence which matched Brian's, she asked, 'Could you please tell us what was the policeman's hat size?'

Once he really did slip up and I think it is the finest tribute to the way people felt about Brian that he got away with it. It was during the Trent Bridge Test of 1980 and England were being held up by one or two stubborn partnerships in the lower regions of the batting order, with Deryck Murray, the wicket-keeper, prominently involved. Brian mentioned the partnerships but then added, 'The nigger in the woodpile is Murray.'

There was a sharp intake of breath all around the commentary box; we looked at each other in disbelief. This was the most politically incorrect figure of speech ever uttered in the history of cricket commentary – and it came from a man who would rather die than be unpleasant, or even impolite, to one of his fellow creatures. It was, of course, an entirely innocent slip of the tongue. It would never occur to BJ, in any circumstances, to be offensive. And, as if the whole world understood this, we received not one letter or phone call of complaint.

His irrepressible sense of humour caused him to poke gentle fun at every one of us at one time or another, and every newcomer to the box – such as overseas broadcasters – could expect to receive his share of it. Alan McGilvray, from Australia, Alan Richards (New Zealand), Tony Cozier (West Indies), Norman Oliver (Australia, after McGillers' retirement), Mushtaq Mohammad and Khalid ('Billy') Ibadulla . . . they all took it well. They, like everyone else, loved Brian, and knew the man was incapable of malice, or even of an unkind thought.

If Brian actively disliked anyone in the whole wide world, he kept it well hidden. I thought I detected, at one time, a bit of antipathy towards two players, but I shall not mention their names. I may have been mistaken. Brian was not a man one associated with dislike or unpleasantness.

His laughter, open or half-suppressed, was infectious and affected us all on occasions. It seemed to affect Don Mosey more than most, and he was understandably affronted when Brian, in a book, described him as 'the worst giggler in the box'. We all knew that that title belonged to BJ himself.

Cakes and sweets used to be delivered to the box by the hundredweight, and John Arlott, for one, was not too keen on this. Once, in a box overflowing with confectionery of all kinds, he turned to me and grunted, 'What do you make of all this?'

Another time, I remember, Brian remarked that a little liquid refreshment would not go amiss with some sort of food which had arrived, and within a couple of hours – at the luncheon interval – a knock at the door signalled the arrival of a delivery boy from Harrods . . . with the required liquid refreshments. The following Monday a parcel arrived for each of us – two bottles of champagne from a listener in France.

Brian himself used to feign bewilderment. 'Aren't people kind?' he would ask. 'Why do you think people send us all these goodies?'

Don told him, a trifle tartly, 'Because you solicit the damn things whenever you are commentating.'

'Do you really think so?' asked Brian, as though the thought had never occurred to him.

He once completed an over of commentary and, while I summarised, turned his attention to a large chocolate cake which had arrived. He accidentally let it fall and I caught the cake, placed it safely on the table and carried on my summary as if nothing had happened. Brian was quite impressed by this.

The letters used to pour in for Brian, and any he did not answer on the air he took home and replied to in his spare time. I think we all adopted the philosophy that if someone took the trouble to write a letter to us, the least we could do was answer it, and Brian set the example.

Brian loved his family, of course. He loved his little Yorkshire terrier, Mini (or perhaps Minnie – I never asked for the spelling); he loved cricket and he loved Lord's. He seemed to love his fellow men and women without exception. In fact I can't think of many people he didn't love. And everyone seemed to love Brian, in return.

Brian never seemed to have aged a day since his schooldays, until, that is, we reached the 1990s. I shared a taxi with him after attending Reg Hayter's birthday (a renowned freelance cricket correspondent) and, for the first time, I thought the old boy was at last beginning to show his age. He confessed that the annual dinner circuit was beginning to get a bit too much for him and said he was going to give it up. Perhaps he was right: perhaps his time had come. He had been born two years before the First World War, and had served gallantly in the Second.

Brian made friends everywhere he went, all over the world, during the whole of his life. I can't think of any doors which were closed to him, anywhere. He had informed, entertained and amused people everywhere he had gone or wherever he had been heard.

Brian Johnston, OBE MC, was a complete and wonderful human being. The years I spent in the company of Jonners and Arlott were among the most rewarding of my life.

13

Great West Indians

George Alphonso Headley was a legend in West Indian cricket before I was born, and yet I actually bowled against him, and in a Test match, too.

He had first played for Jamaica in 1927, and before he was twenty-one he made 176 on his Test debut against England in Barbados (1929–30). In the Third Test of that series, still only twenty years old, he made a century in each innings, and in Australia a year later he scored 102 out of a West Indian total of 193, so that by the time he made his first appearance in England in 1933 he was known as 'the black Bradman'.

It would not be politically correct nowadays to confer such a title, but I've no doubt it was accepted at the time as the highest compliment which could be paid. In fact I mentioned this to a West Indian friend when it was known that Headley was going to play against us in January 1954, and he grinned: 'Over here, man, we call Bradman "the white Headley".'

Well, I had never been able to bowl at Bradman; here was my chance to have a go at his West Indian 'twin', the man who to this day occupies third place in Test batting averages. Headley was now forty-four years old, however, and by the end of that game I was thinking to myself that it was a pity – no, an absolute tragedy – that he should be forced, by weight of public opinion, to carry on and end a wonderful career when his age had slowed him down. There had been an enormous clamour for his recall, especially in Jamaica, where the first Test of 1954 was to be played. I was a bit quick in those days, especially on West Indies pitches, and, in a two-day match before the Test, I hit Headley on the forearm. He was hurt pretty badly and had to go off to receive medical attention. I thought I was going to be lynched.

It was a match played in an exceedingly volatile atmosphere, with crowd demonstrations about everything, not to mention the 'calling' of Tony Lock for throwing his quicker ball – the first time that had been done in a Test for well over fifty years. As a first taste of cricket in the Caribbean, it was a salutory and at times frightening experience for the twenty-three-year-old FST. Happily, I was to have many more pleasant and enjoyable times there.

Of the three Ws – Frank Worrell, Everton Weekes and Clyde Walcott – I found Worrell the best technician and stylist, Weekes the most efficient destroyer of attacks, and Walcott the hardest hitter of the ball off the back foot I have ever seen. I was to see an awful lot of those three.

I can't remember ever having much conversation with Walcott. He was a good wicket-keeper in his younger days, although he was, physically, a big man. I shall remember as long as I live a shot he hit off Tony Lock. Tony got half a hand to it, but the ball still hurtled to the boundary, first bounce. It was possibly the greatest back-foot shot I have ever seen any batsman play.

Frank was a man who enjoyed his cricket and almost always *looked* like he was enjoying it, which made him friends everywhere, amongst players and spectators alike. We played together in one of the earliest games of floodlit cricket – at Bury football ground in Lancashire – and we both remarked how much the white ball swung in the night air.

I saw Worrell most, I think, in the never-to-be-forgotten

Fourth Test of 1954 in Trinidad, the first to be played on a jute-matting pitch which must have been designed *by* a batsman *for* batsmen. It was as near perfect in character as any I have ever seen or heard about. A total of 1,528 runs were scored on it and only twenty-four wickets fell in six days! Amidst all the carnage, however, it was possible for me to find a bit of sympathy for my old mate Bruce Pairadeau, who batted at number five for the West Indies. He came in behind Holt, who had made 40, Stollmeyer (41), Weekes (206), Worrell (167) and Walcott (124), and was going for a single when I got a long, flat throw back to the wicket-keeper from deep fine-leg, and he was run out for 0!

I bowled 48 overs in that match, Trevor Bailey bowled 44, Tony Lock 73, Jim Laker 50, and even Denis Compton, Tom Graveney and Len Hutton had to turn their arm over at one time or another. Brian Statham got it right: he pulled a rib muscle on the first day, after nine overs, and was unable to bowl again in the match.

Everton de Courcy Weekes was the most unorthodox of the three Ws – he was the West Indian Denis Compton in that respect – and was known to us as the Butcher, because of the ferocious efficiency with which he cut the ball. He cut you from anywhere, given the chance. He was always kind enough to say that I gave him more trouble than any other pace bowler because I moved the ball *away*, late and at speed, and that's a rather difficult delivery to cut. He was a truly magnificent batsman. We had many a duel, and in our different ways, we both enjoyed them.

At Edgbaston, in 1957, I bowled Everton for 9 in the first innings and caught him, off Lock, in the second for 33. At Lord's, three weeks later, it was Everton's turn, and although West Indies were beaten comfortably, he played a marvellous innings of 90 in circumstances not many people knew about at the time. Bowling from the Nursery End, I hit Everton on the hand, and after that I noticed that he changed his glove several times. At last, after one such change, I walked over and asked what the trouble was, and he showed me the damaged hand, with blood seeping out from the fingernails. He didn't retire hurt, however, but soldiered on, trying to save the game – and he hit me, off leg-and-middle, on to the grandstand balcony for six.

We went to Trent Bridge for the Third Test where Statham bowled 70 overs, I bowled 65 and Laker bowled 105. It knackered Brian for the season and Lancashire ordered him – didn't *ask* him – to take an extended rest. Yorkshire, on the other hand, ordered me to Hull to play in the next county championship match. Not for the first time, I noticed a slight difference in the man-management of the two counties!

As for Weekes, he went to The Oval and bagged a pair on his last Test appearance against England. It was a game in which Laker and Lock bowled England to an innings victory, but I couldn't help feeling Everton's Test record deserved a happier ending. Sure enough, the following winter, back he came with 197, 78, 24, 39, 41, 16 not out, 51 and 9 against

Pakistan. By this time, however, a new West Indian hero was emerging . . .

Garfield St Aubrun Sobers was a lean, lithe young man we had first come across at Sabina Park, Jamaica, at the end of March 1954, and to be frank, no one had taken much notice of a chap who bowled a bit of slow left-arm and batted at number nine. Little did we, or anyone else outside the West Indies for that matter, realise that he was to become the greatest of modern all-rounders, a cricketer of such dazzling talent and versatile athleticism that he would cause people all over the world to start throwing away their record books. On that first encounter I labelled him a man who looked as though he could *become* a decent cricketer, and thought no more about him. He scored 14 not out and 26 in Jamaica and his first Test wicket was, ironically, that of Trevor Bailey, who would one day write a biography of the great all-rounder.

I tried Gary out with a bouncer in that game in Jamaica and he ducked into it. Later he told me he had vowed, in that moment, never to duck to a bouncer again. I don't know whether he kept his word, but he certainly got a bigger reputation than any of his contemporaries for hooking bouncers. It was well merited, although, just occasionally, it got him into trouble.

At The Oval in 1966, England, 3–1 down in the series in which they were captained first by Mike Smith and then by Colin Cowdrey, called up Brian Close to lead them in the final Test. Closey didn't talk *to* the opposition in any intimidatory way, but he was not averse to talking *about* them – and quite audibly, too. He knew full well that Gary had played a major part in the series so far (722 runs at an average of 103, 20 wickets and 10 catches), so he told John Snow to greet the West Indies captain with a bouncer, airily remarking to John Murray, the wicket-keeper, that if Gary got an edge on the off-side, the catch was Murray's, and if it came on the leg-side, Closey would do the necessary. With that he took up his position in one of his kamikaze spots at short leg.

Gary listened to the chat with more than casual interest. Down came the bouncer and he hooked – before he had given himself any time at all to judge the pace of the pitch or anything else. I think almost anyone else I have ever known would have ducked as Sobers was seen to position himself for the hook, but not Closey. The ball struck the bottom edge, hit Gary in the 'box', and there was Closey to take the catch. Thank you very much. Gary, magnificent sportsman that he was, mystified the crowd by departing, laughing, for a first-ball duck.

That was the nature of the man. Every game he played in was a contest – but it was a contest of joyousness, of revelling in pitting his colossal talent against that of others. If I ever bounced him with a long-leg or deep square-leg positioned, he would turn away, let the ball go by and laugh at me: 'Not today, Freddie . . . not today.' It was the same in everything he did: on the golf course he was a tiger, but a decent, honorable tiger. I am quite certain he would have agreed to play a round with Jack Nicklaus for a fiver with no handicaps involved. I've played many a round with Gary and he was always the same – he played like a demon, but with a laugh and a sense of sheer enjoyment. He could, I think, play any game with the same unaffected sense of enjoyment. Quite simply, he loves life and he lives it to the full.

Gary scored 226 against us in Barbados in 1960, and when he and Frankie Worrell had put on 399 for the fourth wicket, we were just about in despair. I asked Peter May if I could go round the wicket and he agreed: 'Might as well try it.' I promptly knocked out Gary's middle stump. In the next Test, in Trinidad, I went round the wicket as soon as Gary came in, and did him either first or second ball. Over dinner with Frankie Worrell and Wes Hall, Gary told me that a bowler of my pace should not be allowed to bowl round the wicket into the rough but I was never quite sure whether he was joking or not.

That was an amazing Test. There was a record crowd of 30,000 – the biggest for any sporting occasion in the West Indies – and Wes and his opening partner, Chester Watson, were warned by both umpires for intimidation with fast, short-pitched bowling. Then there was a complete riot which halted play for the day when the debutant Cheran Singh was run out shortly after tea. Life was never dull on a West Indies tour.

It's not widely known that Gary once played for Yorkshire. It's quite true – I've won money on it. In 1964 Yorkshire went on a privately arranged tour of Canada and the USA, ending up in Bermuda, where I was told Gary was arriving and was asked if I would pick him up at the airport. Gary was expected to play for Bermuda in the match which had been arranged, but he insisted, 'I'm not playing *against* you lot, but I wouldn't mind playing with you.' So that was settled, and off we went to a nightclub, where Gary, you might say, enjoyed to the full most of the pleasures that are available in Bermuda.

He did not look well the following morning; in fact he looked distinctly seedy. He scored a century, however, then took the new ball and added five wickets to his contribution. The man really was quite unbelievable. Never have I encountered such all-round talent in such abundance.

Last year the phone rang and a voice from Ilkley Golf Club said, 'Gary Sobers is here and would love to see you.' I immediately drove the ten miles over to Ilkley for the sort of joyous reunion we have always had. Gary sent me a letter recently asking me to play in a golf day he was organising for this summer somewhere in Notts. I'll be there . . .

14

John Brian Statham CBE

Statham played 430 matches for Lancashire between 1950 and 1968, and 70 Tests for England, taking 252 wickets at 24.84. He captained Lancashire in his last three seasons and was awarded the CBE during that period.

'George' Statham and I have been friends for over forty years and not one wrong word has ever passed between us. This is little short of remarkable when I think of the number of people who have tried to drive a wedge between us – either by accident or, in some cases, by cynical design. I have become quite sick of the number of times I have been told, 'You *needed* Statham at the other end.' It just isn't true, any more than one can say Brian *needed* me, or anyone else for that matter, at the opposite end.

The plain truth is that the two of us operated in tandem in barely half the Tests either of us played: we enjoyed the luxury of opening the bowling together in five successive Tests only against South Africa in 1960 and on tour in Australia in 1962. In between I had partners like Alec Bedser, Trevor Bailey, Peter

Loader, Frank Tyson, Alan Moss, Harold Rhodes, Les Jackson, Len Coldwell, David Larter, Derek Shackleton, Jack Flavell, John Price and Fred Rumsey. Brian, for his part, was partnered by Bedser, Fred Ridgway, Bailey, Tyson, Loader, Flavell and David Brown.

We were contrasting types as well as contrasting bowlers: I relied largely on late swing; Brian relied on top-notch accuracy and movement of the ball off the seam. If he ever swung a ball (as he will tell you) it was by accidental use of atmospheric conditions. Brian was quiet to the point of diffidence; I told people what I thought, and if they didn't like it, that was too bad. It was a bit like the detectives in films who interrogate suspects in pairs: good guy, bad guy.

The simple fact was that neither of us particularly cared who took the wickets so long as the opposition were being bowled out. We have always liked and respected each other, as men and as cricketers, and that has been good enough for both of us. If a third party has ever attempted to 'knock' one of us to the other – and you'd be surprised how many have – then invariably it has been stopped in double-quick time. We have always looked out for each other.

'George' was without doubt one of England's finest ever fast bowlers. I used to marvel that he could generate such pace from what I regarded as a slight frame, but he was wiry and he was supple. He liked his beer as much as the next man and more than most, although he never seemed to put on an ounce of weight. His fondness for ale, however, did affect him in other ways. I once found him in our room in the West Indies fast asleep and snoring with the air conditioning going full blast – and 'George', dead to the world, was turning blue with cold!

It was in Guyana that 'George', with 'Noddy' Pullar, Tommy Greenhough and myself, went to the cinema. A girl came round with a tray of chocolate, sweets, cigarettes and matches and asked if we wanted anything. 'Yes,' said Brian. 'Four cold cans of lager . . . and bring four more every time you come to this part of the cinema.' We became quite lively as the show went on, especially when an announcement was flashed on to the screen: 'England cricketers Ken Barrington and Ray Illingworth are here watching the film.' It wasn't a case of mistaken identity – Kenny and Raymond were in another part of the cinema. It must have been their most expensive day out of the tour, because they both usually kept a tight hold on their purse-strings!

On tour in Australia in 1958–9 we went together to see Nat King Cole in concert at the Hilton Hotel. It was a sell-out, naturally, but the Hilton management very kindly set up a table in an alcove which would otherwise have been curtained off, and so we were able to see that great entertainer, and to meet him afterwards, too.

I missed 'George' as a companion on the boat trip to Australia for the 1962–3 tour because he couldn't get away at the time we sailed. However, he flew out, and when we docked at Fremantle, there was 'George' on the dockside to greet us. It was a great reunion.

We moved on to Adelaide and I remember the two of us attending a party there. The party was just breaking up at a late hour when Brian carried out his own investigation of the beer supply.

'Hold on a minute,' he said, as everyone was in the process of leaving, 'there's a barrel here which isn't empty yet.' And the party resumed. The following morning, ironically, we were both given the congratulations of the management on being two of the first players on parade. Little did they know we hadn't been to bed at all.

The Rev. David Sheppard had had one or two catching lapses so far on the tour, which were all the more poignant to me because they had occurred when he was fielding at short fine-leg, a position I regarded very definitely as mine. I couldn't field there to my own bowling, of course, and so the future Bishop of Liverpool was occasionally to be found there. Eventually his mistakes caused him to be moved to *deep* fine-leg, and it was there that his moment of triumph came . . . or so he thought. Fred Titmus dropped one short, the batsman hooked, and Sheppard, on the boundary, held the catch. In a frenzy of delight, he hurled the ball high into the air and, as he waited for the ball to return to his hands, the voice of J. B. Statham was heard from neighbouring third man: 'You'd better chuck it in, Rev. It was a no-ball and they're on their third run!'

It's fair to say, I think, that the friendship between the two of us has grown steadily as the years have gone by, especially since we both retired from the game. Brian has always supported my charity golf days; I have been glad to help him whenever it has been necessary. To use a popular modern phrase, we are always there for each other, and I feel sure that will always be the case. I was delighted when Brian's presidency of Lancashire County Cricket Club was announced, and it will be my very great pleasure to take wine with him in the committee room at Old Trafford during the Roses match.

15

Pals and Personalities

Graham Anthony Richard Lock was a Surrey and England cricketer with the heart of a lion, a fear of absolutely nothing at all and an unswerving loyalty to any and every captain he played under. He died in 1995 from throat cancer.

When I first saw Lockie in action at The Oval he had a full head of red hair. He lost much of it prematurely, and the abiding memory of most people will be of a balding man, full of fire and aggression as a bowler, and a catcher of breathtaking brilliance. I have watched him take catches, close to the wicket or off his own bowling, which I am convinced no one else I have ever seen could have taken.

What a competitor he was! In 1955 when he took 216 wickets (at an average of 14.39) he asked me anxiously, 'When Bob Appleyard took two hundred wickets for Yorkshire in 1951, was it *exactly* two hundred or did he get more?' I reassured him that he had taken more wickets in the season than Appleyard, but couldn't resist adding that Bob's had cost 14.14 each! Lockie simply had to be the best.

As a slow left-armer, I didn't rate him quite as highly as Johnny Wardle, whom I considered a more complete bowler with more variety to his attack. As a competitor, however, no one was ahead of G. A. R. Lock. When you hear about people who eat, drink and live cricket, think of Lockie. He used to dream about it as well – and with the same enthusiasm.

When Jim Laker heard that I was going to room with Lockie on the 1953–4 tour to the West Indies, he said, 'Hard luck.'

'What do you mean?' I asked.

Jim responded, 'You'll see . . .'

It wasn't long before I realised what he meant. In the middle of the night Lockie would rise up in bed, arms outstretched, and roar, 'How's that?' at the top of his voice before sinking back and continuing his sound sleep. It was not quite so easy for his room-mate, especially when, sleep gently beginning to consume him at last, the next interruption came in the shape of a round of applause and a resounding 'Well done . . . great catch' from the once more upright (but still sleeping) Lock.

Lock and Laker, of course, played a major part in Surrey's seven championship successes in the 1950s. Individually, they were magnificent bowlers; as a pair they were devastating and, on a pitch which suited them, irresistible. I am not saying that wickets at The Oval were prepared specifically for them, but Surrey would have been mad to present pitches which hindered Lock and Laker, wouldn't they? In comparing Surrey's successes in the fifties with Yorkshire, therefore, it's important to bear in mind that while Surrey performed regularly at The Oval, Yorkshire had to travel round Leeds, Bradford, Sheffield, Hull, Harrogate and Scarborough. The pitches at Headingley and Bramall Lane alone cost us many a championship.

Lock played in 49 Tests and took 174 wickets at 25.58, but that doesn't even tell half the story. When I first saw him, Tony bowled what I called slow left-arm 'lollipops'. Although he undoubtedly spun the ball a great deal, he bowled at a gentle pace. About five years into his career at Surrey he started to speed up to something like medium pace and bowled a faster ball which really was fast. At Kingston (Jamaica) in 1954, he bowled George Headley with a quicker one which absolutely dumbfounded that great West Indian. Headley just stood there for a minute with a look of absolute bewilderment on his face, and Godfrey Evans said to him, 'If you had been just a second *later* you would have middled it.'

Lock was utterly shattered to be 'called' for throwing during that Test. I remember him in our room that evening, still white and shaking – he was physically upset, not just mentally. It happened again with a number of different umpires, and Lock eventually reverted to his early style of slow, flighted deliveries.

I was given a glimpse of what his quicker ball was like at Alec Bedser's benefit match at The Oval, for which I got leave from the RAF. In due course, I faced Lockie. He bowled one which pitched in the rough, took off and just grazed my chin. I can remember it quite clearly forty years later – like someone tickling me with a feather. It hit Arthur McIntyre on the shoulder, whistled past Peter May's head at slip and went for four byes with no one getting anywhere near it.

The quicker ball wasn't the only one that got him into trouble, either. Lockie had a pronounced drag – in fact he was the only slow bowler I ever saw who had a fast bowler's drag-plate on his left (rear) boot.

Whatever his faults, he gave a hundred per cent to every team and every captain he played for. I remember being given a lift part of the way home from Old Trafford by Len Hutton after the Old Trafford Test of 1952. Lockie had made his debut in the game and hadn't bowled at all in the first innings but in the second he had taken 4 for 36. I mentioned to Leonard that he had a funny action.

Hutton smiled that enigmatic little smile which was very much his trademark and murmered, 'Aye, I think I might beat t'Australians with him next year.' In 1953 we played four draws against the Aussies, and at The Oval we won by eight wickets with Lock taking 5 for 45 and Laker 4 for 75 in the second innings.

I think Lockie was a little bit disillusioned when he was left out of the party to tour Australia in 1962–3, and he went out to spend his winter playing for Western Australia, at that time the poor relation of Australian cricket – Perth did not get a Test match in those days. Lockie continued to play there for the next nine winters and utterly transformed cricket in the state. He led them to a Sheffield Shield title, bowled some of the best stuff of his entire career and, even more to the point, watched the development of Dennis Lillee, who was to become one of Australia's finest fast bowlers. If for nothing else, the world should thank Tony Lock for that, although there was so much more to him . . .

He joined Leicestershire in 1965 (while continuing to winter in Australia), and skippered them in 1966 and 1967, taking them to second place in the county championship in '67 – their best-ever season up to that time. I believe he laid the foundations for the better days to come.

It was Lock's achievements in Australia and the way he had rejuvenated Leicestershire which brought his recall to the England side to tour West Indies in 1967–8. It gave him the chance to bow out of Test cricket in the grand manner . . . but not quite as people expected. At Bourda (Guyana) he made his highest Test score (89) on his last appearance and partnered 'Percy' Pocock in a stand of 109 for the ninth wicket.

It was not, of course, as a batsman that one remembers Tony Lock; it was not, in my case, entirely as a bowler that I remember him, though he could bowl on any kind of pitch and make the batsman work. When I think of Lockie I think of the fieldsman . . . the competitor. As clearly as if it was happening now, I can see him bowl a full toss to Len Hutton at The Oval in the 1950s. Hutton drove it on the on-side, very hard, and about as high as Leonard ever hit the ball in the air – less than six feet. Lockie took off, dived to his right and held the catch in his right hand, which was, of course, the 'wrong' hand. It was probably the greatest caught-and-bowled I ever saw.

Lindwall and Miller, Ramadhin and Valentine, and I like to think Statham and Trueman . . . these have been some of

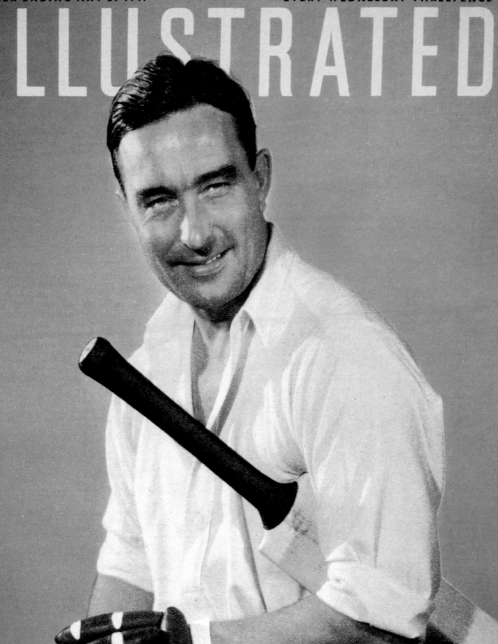

WEEK ENDING MAY 21 1949   EVERY WEDNESDAY THREEPENCE

ILLUSTRATED

THIS YEAR OF COMPTON

The Brylcreem Boy of 1947 – Denis Compton.

An heroic figure of the post-war years – Keith Miller.

Frank Worrell despatches one to the
mid-wicket boundary.

Everton Weekes, 40 years on.

'Johnners'

Len Hutton – England's first
professional captain.

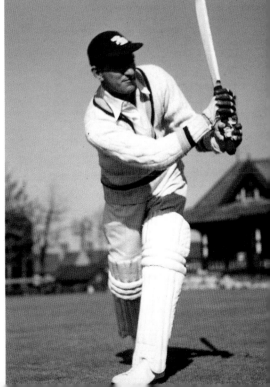

Gary Sobers – the greatest of modern all-rounders.

Three promising golfers (and not bad cricketers, either): Ian Botham, Brian Lara and Gary Sobers.

An innings from Ian Botham could transform a Test match.

Don Mosey, 'the Alderman,' on Test Match Special duty with Tony Cozier and Terry Lewis.

The TMS team of 1980: standing; Tony Lewis, Henry Blofeld, Ray Illingworth, Chris Martin-Jenkins, Peter Baxter, Bill Frindall. Seated; Don Mosey, Trevor Bailey, Brian Johnston, F.S.T., Tony Cozier (absent: John Arlott).

Darren Gough builds up a head of steam.

Mike Atherton in 1997, scoring a century against the Australians in the Oval One Day International

Ted Dexter and David Gower in reflective mood.

Mike Atherton in 1995, after scoring 185 to save England in the Johannesburg Test against South Africa.

F.S.T. with Don Bradman – the greatest batsman of them all.

the great post-war pairings of bowlers, together with Laker and Lock.

Dennis Brian Close was born eighteen days after me. We went on our first Yorkshire Federation tour together aged seventeen (and made sufficient impact in our game against Sussex for them to ask Yorkshire for 'first refusal' if we should prove surplus to requirements in our native county), and we played our first games for Yorkshire together against Cambridge University in May 1949.

Closey, as he has always been known throughout the game, never fulfilled completely one of the greatest cricketing talents I have ever seen. At first, he batted left-hand and bowled a lively fast-medium pace with a beautiful outswinger, and if he had been left alone, who knows what he might have achieved. He was most assuredly a better new-ball bowler than anyone around today. Yorkshire, however, thought they had unearthed another Frank Smailes (left-hand bat, right-arm medium pace and off-spin bowler of the 1930s) and encouraged Closey to develop as an off-break bowler. Nevertheless, he still scored nearly 35,000 runs, took well over 1,100 wickets, held more than 800 catches and even stumped one man during his career with Yorkshire, Somerset and England.

Like most other people who have known him well, I had a love–hate relationship with Closey. He had this enormous God-given talent, and one of the finest cricket brains of all time, and yet when it came down to plain, simple common sense, I have known him to do the daftest things imaginable! There were times when he drove me – and others – to despair.

Above all else, though, I am utterly convinced that if Closey had played for himself, rather than for the team, he would have set more records than he did. As a captain – Yorkshire 1963–70 and Somerset 1972–7, England 1966–7 – he gave absolutely everything he had to his side. That Yorkshire team of the 1960s . . . we would have followed him anywhere. Mind you, we would probably have lynched him when we ultimately found ourselves in some lunatic situation – but we would have won the game first!

There were times when it has to be conceded that Closey was a bit unlucky. He never reached 200 in an innings, for instance, but at The Oval, in 1960, he was on 198 when he saw Ron Tindall, one of the most athletic outfielders in the game, race yards round the boundary to bring off a spectacular catch.

Only a few weeks later he had reached 180 against Notts at Scarborough, when he saw Mervyn Winfield complete another outstanding chasing catch on the boundary. Insult was added to injury when the bowler, 'Bomber' Wells, grinned at him as a seriously disgruntled D. B. Close trudged off the field: 'Ah, Closey, you always were a sucker for my leg trap.'

In the dressing-room we retreated to every corner and hiding-place we could find. The bat hit the back wall with a force that nearly caused the pavilion to collapse, and one glove went through an open window and ended up in the road outside the ground!

Once again at The Oval, Brian drove a ball from Lock, quite fiercely. He set off for a run, only to find that Lockie, following up, had picked up the ball and thrown the wicket down in one movement. It didn't help when Roy Swetman, the wicket-keeper, grinned at him and said, 'Even *that* pitched leg-and-middle and hit off, Closey.'

God in His goodness compensates for these things, however: in Close's case, it was with his recently developed off-spin-cum-medium-pace bowling, including what we called 'the tactical full toss', or sometimes the 'tactical long hop'. Whichever one it was, Closey was your man to break an unexpected and stubborn partnership. He could usually account for Ted Dexter, one of the most gifted batsmen in the world at the time, with the full toss. Dexter used to have nightmares about the way he got out to Closey.

Arthur Milton was once proving troublesome at Bristol, and Brian was introduced to the attack. Jimmy Binks said to the batsman, 'Hard luck,' and Arthur asked what he meant. Jimmy replied that he didn't know how it would happen, but without any doubt the batsman's downfall was nigh. Sure enough, down came a short-pitched ball, Milton pulled lustily, and Don Wilson held the catch at midwicket. When Bernie Constable was going well at The Oval, and we didn't seem able to shift him, I suggested to Norman Yardley, 'Put "Wonder Boy" on.' Bernie, well past his 50 at this time, hooked the third ball. It hit Yardley in the middle of the back and Hutton caught the rebound at slip.

As a fieldsman, Closey had no sense of fear whatsoever: he put himself in positions which had never been seen in cricket before, and if the batsman hit him – whether it was on the shin or the head – he would snarl at the horrified bowler, 'Get on with it. We've got to win this bloody game.' The folklore of the game is littered with stories of that kind, all absolutely true.

The way Closey was treated by Yorkshire was nothing less than totally disgraceful. He was given ten minutes to make up his mind whether to resign or be sacked – another of A. B. Sellers' masterpieces of man-management – after leading Yorkshire to four county championships and two Gillette Cup wins in eight years.

If Closey had faults, then we, the men who played alongside him, were the ones who had the right to say so. I have heard people in the south criticise Closey, and told them, 'When he wakes up tomorrow morning he will have more cricketing knowledge in his little finger than you'll ever acquire in a lifetime,' and it's true. I've been appalled in recent years at the way the knowledge and experience of Closey, Raymond Illingworth (moaner though he was and always has been, he knew his stuff) and Don Kenyon, of Worcestershire, has been neglected. It has all been thrown away, ignored.

When it comes to common sense, however . . . well, that's something else altogether, and nowhere was Closey more of an idiot than when he was behind the wheel of a car. It started, I think, when he had a grey Humber Hawk: we were in London and a policeman arrived at the ground to say that someone had driven into the car. Closey, in pads and gloves, went out from the nets to look at it and returned cursing heartily. He then drove around with the car door fastened up with string for a time until the car dealers loaned him another Humber while his was repaired.

No sooner had Closey acquired his replacement car than we were playing the Australians at Bradford, and, as usual, it rained all the first day. With no play possible, some of the Aussies asked if we could arrange a round of golf, and Closey said, 'Leave it to me.' Golf was fixed up at the Halifax club, out on the moors at Ogden. Lindwall, Miller and co. arrived there . . . but no Closey. They waited . . . and waited . . . until ultimately he arrived (cursing, of course) to report that he had had a collision with a lorry-load of firewood. The lorry, with its load, had been knocked off the road and down an embankment. Closey (as he always does) emerged without a scratch and there

was a certain amusement in the Yorkshire dressing-room when, in the subsequent court case, he was completely exonerated: 'he had been driving at thirty miles an hour.' Now that was strange. None of us had ever known him to drive at thirty miles an hour, even from a standing start!

So it has continued over the years, although it has to be said that he has been unlucky . . . trees leap out of forests and savage his motorcars without warning; borough surveyors dig holes in main roads without taking the trouble to inform D. B. Close. Don Mosey and I have built up a dossier on Brian's highway adventures which we have often thought of turning into a book, but it wouldn't be one for bedtime reading to the children.

All that apart, he led a team in the sixties of proud Yorkshiremen and every one of them would tell you Closey would die rather than lose a match which there was even a faint possibility of winning. A couple of umpires at Lord's once said there was an air of efficiency and a sense of purpose about Yorkshire going out on to the field which was worth three wickets' start. David Lloyd, later captain of Lancashire and subsequently England coach, once told me that the very sight of Yorkshire filing in for lunch in their blazers had 'frightened him to death'.

How sad, how terribly sad, that things have changed. Closey hasn't, however. After the way he left the county, it took a pretty big man to come back and serve on the committee, for much of the time as cricket chairman, but he did it. The club, the team, was always greater than any individual to Closey. He was picked and dropped by England eight times; he captained England seven times without losing but was again discarded, for reasons completely divorced from Test cricket. Yet at the age of forty-five he came back, when England called, to open the batting against Andy Roberts, Michael Holding and Wayne Daniel on a sub-standard pitch. For sheer guts, I can't think there have been many like him.

Amongst the several towering personalities in county cricket when I joined the circuit, none was more impressive than Wilfred

Wooller, though it seemed to me that we were destined to get off on the wrong foot right from the start.

In my first game against Glamorgan, at Neath, I heard him saying to spectators in front of the dressing-rooms, 'Now just look at this chap . . . look at where that back foot is when he delivers the ball. That's how they train them to bowl in Yorkshire.' It's true that I had a pronounced 'drag'. Nevertheless, I wasn't too impressed by this.

I asked some of the senior players about the bloke who was doing the 'knocking', and learned that Wooller, captain of Glamorgan, was a public schoolboy, a Cambridge graduate and a wartime officer in the Royal Artillery. It all seemed to add up to the sort of figure that a Yorkshireman from the working-classes, *and* a fast bowler as well, was destined to regard as a natural enemy. I resolved that when he came in to bat in the second innings I would tickle him up a bit . . .

It was only later, during a long period of close acquaintance, that I learned that there was much, much more to Wilf Wooller than the simple details of his background. He was a giant of a man in almost every way. He was very, very tough, a born fighter and a natural leader. He gave everything he had to every game for Glamorgan and could be very hard indeed on anyone he felt was not doing the same. After his death in March 1997, one obituarist wrote, 'He hardly suffered fools at all, let alone gladly,' and I couldn't help feeling that was absolutely right.

After that first encounter with Wooller, I was prepared for a lifelong tussle with the man, sentiments which lasted no longer than a few hours. At close of play on the first day of that game he came into the Yorkshire dressing-room and brusquely addressed me: 'Come on. Get yourself showered and changed. We are going out to dinner.'

Bewildered, because I was, remember, a raw eighteen-year-old from the South Yorkshire coalfields, I dressed and joined him. We went off for dinner with his wife, Enid, and Wilf told me, 'You have a beautiful action and I don't see any reason why you shouldn't become England's spearhead for the next ten years.' We sat and talked cricket until one o'clock in the morning. I never thought of Wilf Wooller as 'the enemy' again. A tough opponent, yes. A grim, fighting adversary, yes. A man I wanted to beat as badly as he wanted to beat me, yes. But a man I respected totally and wholeheartedly.

I learned much about Wilf Wooller in the years that followed: how he had been an outstanding centre three-quarter for Wales (one of the greatest ever, it was said) . . . how he had been taken prisoner by the Japanese in Java . . . how, in only his second season as captain of Glamorgan, he had taken a team of nine Welshmen and a couple of players who were 'surplus to requirements' elsewhere and forged a championship-winning side.

It was a success which staggered just about everybody else in first-class cricket, and was achieved more than anything else through his leadership by example. Wilf somehow created a corps of brilliant close-to-the-wicket catchers, and his bowlers, who could really be described only as moderately gifted, suddenly found themselves taking more wickets than they had ever imagined possible. Right in the forefront of the close-catchers was the powerful figure of W. Wooller.

Wilf was no mean performer himself with bat and ball. His 13,856 runs were averaged at 22, and his fast-medium bowling brought him just short of 1,000 wickets at 26. He also held 412 catches, mostly when fielding in suicidal positions a yard or two from the bat. He would never ask anyone to do anything he was not prepared to do himself, and thus he was usually to be found at short-leg, very much like D. B. Close.

It was a case of leading from the front again when he played a prominent part in the memorable Welsh rugby victory over the All Blacks in 1935, and he celebrated in typical rugby fashion by heaving a piano over an hotel's banisters.

His attitude to life was as forthright and uncompromising as his approach on the cricket or rugby field. He spoke his mind, said what he thought, and if it offended the person he was addressing – well, too bad. With Wilf Wooller, it was truly 'what you saw was what you got'.

It must not be thought, however, that he was a hulking, bullying brute of a man. He was a deep thinker about both games. I never discussed rugby with him, but I did spend many hours talking cricket, and, especially in my very young days, he opened my eyes to many aspects of my game. He would go through the country's leading batsmen and detail the way they held the bat, the position of top hand as well as bottom. He knew the positioning of batsmen's feet and their initial movements and gave deep thought to the positioning of fieldsmen, with the strengths and weaknesses of the opposing batsman very much in mind – as all the great captains have done.

I very much doubt whether the words 'defeat' or 'surrender' ever entered his mind. He would resist to the very end in any game he played, yet he had a keen, if mordant, sense of humour which is perhaps best illustrated by a story which went the rounds in the 1950s. Glamorgan were playing at Bristol and, on a brilliant summer day, toiled for six hours in the field while Gloucestershire piled up well over 400 runs for, I think, four wickets. Then the weather changed, and as he stood having a drink in the bar afterwards with the opposition captain, George Emmett, Wilf suggested they retire for a meal.

'I can't,' replied George. 'I must stand here and listen to the sound of the rain falling on the roof of this pavilion. It is a strange and lovely sound of music.'

Wilf had little patience with such rhapsodic reflections and again suggested a move. 'Not yet,' mused George. 'I want to think of the feelings of my spin bowlers as they, too, hear the music of the falling rain and prepare for that beautiful sticky wicket they will find tomorrow morning.' (Uncovered pitches in those days, of course.)

Arriving at the ground the following morning, Wooller was met by Emmett, who announced, 'We have declared at our overnight score.'

'I thought you might,' answered Wilf, tersely, and retired to rally his troops.

'Now this is the plot,' he told Glamorgan. 'It's a rather

different pitch from the one we bowled on yesterday. If we can somehow manage a lead of 120 or 130, it will have become unplayable. Then we can really get at 'em and win by an innings.'

The Glamorgan batsmen clearly did not share their captain's optimism, but no one ventured a different view. You didn't, with Wilf Wooller. Just over an hour later Glamorgan were all out for 38 and Sam Cook, the slow left-arm bowler, had taken six wickets.

'I'd like you to follow on,' said George Emmett.

Wooller responded, 'I thought you might,' and retired to address his troops once more – an even more subdued bunch.

'It's now a different story,' Wooller told them. 'We have to follow on, but we can still win this game. The top will have gone completely by the time they have to bat again. A lead of even ninety should be enough to give us the chance we need.'

No one dared to look him in the eye but someone mumbled, 'We'll do our best, Skip.'

'I know you will,' replied the captain, 'otherwise you won't be playing in this side again.'

The second innings started and went in a roughly similar fashion to the the first one. Wooller went out to bat with the scoreboard showing 26 for 6, and on his way to the wicket he passed Sam Cook who, you might say, was looking quietly confident.

Wooller paused and snarled at him, 'I suppose you'd like to bowl at this circus of mine every day of your life, wouldn't you?' Sam, with ten wickets in the match already under his belt, said nothing. Wooller, face like thunder, marched to the wicket and growled, 'Give me two leg, umpire.' He slammed his bat down hard enough to strike oil before looking up to call to the bowler, 'Come on, Cookie, now let's really see what you are made of.'

Sam trotted in, flighted the ball; it pitched, bounced, turned, hit Wilf on the glove, and short-leg took the catch: 26 for 7. As Wooller walked away, back past the bowler, Sam

enjoyed his moment of triumph: 'Cheerio, Ringmaster,' he grinned.

Charles Bowmar Harris was well into the veteran stage when I first encountered him – he was over forty; I was under twenty – but I knew *of* him, of course, as everyone in the game knew of the practical joker and genial eccentric who had been Nottinghamshire's opening batsman since 1928.

Jim Laker used to tell how Charlie stopped a fast bowler in full cry in his approach to the wicket with the explanation: 'You have an extra fieldsman in the gulley.' The whole game was held up for an investigation to be made and it was then discovered that Harris had placed his false teeth on the ground in roughly the place gulley would stand. Those choppers were a favourite prop of Charlie's. In the 1950s the Trent Bridge pitch was notorious as a bowler's graveyard, a complete 'featherbed' where it was extremely difficult to bowl out any side.

Things had reached such desperation at one stage that the Notts captain, Bill Sime, called upon Charlie to deliver an over or two of his stuff, which so defied description that the reference books refer to it succinctly as 'medium or slow'. Charlie asked his captain for a short-leg fieldsman. Sime was astonished, while the fieldsmen went white and tried to avoid the captain's gaze. No one was going to position himself willingly at 'Boot Hill'. When Sime turned down his bowler's request, therefore, it didn't faze C. B. Harris for a moment. He went to the umpire, borrowed a couple of matches, and propped up the trusty false teeth at short-leg, telling them, 'If anything comes round there, catch it.'

Roy Tattersall, who didn't often stray in line and length, was stopped in mid-run by Charlie, who gravely walked a few paces down the pitch, scraped a mark on the turf with the bottom of his bat and told the astonished 'George', 'If you pitch anything short of there I shall *sweep* you.'

No one escaped his droll humour – and no one resented it. I think every man in every visiting team looked forward to some new caper of Charlie's, because no one ever knew what he might do next. Against Surrey, he put a dolly catch into the air, and as three fieldsmen plus wicket-keeper edged forward – all with an equal chance of making the catch – Charlie trotted gently by and shouted, 'Mine.' Everyone stopped . . . and the ball fell gently to earth. It's the sort of thing you might expect on a village green, but this was a county championship game on a Test match ground!

I took a hat-trick against Notts when Charlie wasn't playing, and he told me afterwards I wouldn't have done it if he had been there. 'How do you make that out?' I asked, and Charlie blithely informed me he would have kept stopping me on my run-in so that I was completely distracted. I'll bet he would have done, too.

He once dived to take a catch off Harold Butler and rolled around the ground in agony, claiming he had broken a bone. It was, in fact, nothing more than a dislocation – painful enough, I suppose – and Charlie was taken to hospital for a precautionary X-ray.

When told it was a minor injury and that the dislocation was to be put back into postion, he enquired, nervously, 'Will it hurt?'

'Not much,' he was told, and the sleeve was rolled up ready for the simple operation. Charlie took a towel, rolled it up tightly and clenched it between his teeth as the collarbone was put back – and he screamed!

A senior nurse, who was, as it happened, an ardent Notts supporter, reproached him severely. 'There's a nineteen-year-old girl just down the corridor who gave birth to twins this morning,' she told him, 'and she didn't make half so much noise as you.'

'Aye,' replied Charlie, 'but just you try putting 'em back.' He liked having the last word.

During the war Charlie played for an Army team, captained by A. B. Sellers, in a match at Lord's. 'You are all soldiers,' Sellers told his team, and this is the world headquarters of cricket. You will all be smart and correct in everything you do.'

Private Harris, C. B., took him at his word. At the end of every over he came smartly to attention and *marched* to his new position. He stopped short of saluting, but only, I suspect, because he was not wearing a cap.

When the players put in their expense claims for that match, Charlie's came to an exorbitant amount and the MCC Secretary looked at it in horror. 'I'm certainly not paying this,' he declared. Then, doing a quick sum in his head, he made his decision: 'I'll pay you six pounds.'

'Done,' said Harris, and shook hands on the deal. He had made a profit.

Another in much the same mould as Charlie Harris was Bryan Douglas Wells, who played for his native Gloucestershire in the fifties and then moved to Notts during the following decade. He had a rich West Country burr and much the same wry sense of humour as Charlie Harris.

Wells bowled off-spinners off a run of no more than two paces, and once told his captain on a hot day at Bradford,

'In this heat, Skipper, if you wants me to bowl another over I s'll 'ave to cut me run down.' He then gravely bowled off *one* step.

He once came in to face a hat-trick ball from me, took guard, gazed earnestly round the field for a long time, then announced to the close-catchers (who comprised the entire team), 'If Fred bowls a straight 'un, I'd say 'e'll 'ave a fair chance.'

His batting was legendary. Against anything faster than a slow left-armer, he would take one step back towards the square-leg umpire and flail with a horizontal bat. The result was that in 302 first-class innings he made a grand total of 2,413 runs. At least six of those came off me . . . with a square cut for six at Worksop. He stepped back and looked at the scoreboard with pride. Everyone laughed, even me. He knew, and I knew he knew, that no bouncer would follow.

Playing cricket in those days could be fun. There was no aggressive sledging, as they call it, but there was banter in abundance. It's sad that the game has lost so much.

Norman Yardley was one of the gentlemen of the game and the best tactical amateur captain I ever played with. He could 'read' a wicket better than anyone else I have ever known. I would reckon that he was right ninety-nine and a half times out of a hundred in predicting how a pitch would play, and this was a tremendous asset to any side he skippered.

It was a great shame that Yorkshire never won a championship for him in the 1950s, because, man for man, that was a magnificent side, but Norman was too nice a person to be tough when toughness was urgently needed. I would also have liked to see him become the second Yorkshire amateur captain to hit 200 in an innings (as Sellers had done in 1936 against Cambridge University), but Norman didn't think about personal records, and was on 183 against Hampshire at Headingley when he declared overnight and deprived himself of the chance.

Those were my early years with Yorkshire, and interesting years they were. We travelled mostly by train, often arriving in the early hours of the morning to snatch a bit of sleep before starting a new game. We once made our way from Dover to Jesmond for a three-day game against Northumberland to learn that the hotel where we expected to stay had been closed three months earlier. Three or four of us had to club together to share one room at the Station Hotel where we could have a bit of a rest for an hour or two before the game started.

On one trip from Yorkshire to Bournemouth we were all a bit surprised to find that the train got as far as Christchurch . . . and terminated. Finding transport in rural Hampshire at three a.m. is no picnic, I can tell you.

In addition to the players, we had two official members of the party in those days – Bright Heyhirst, the masseur, and Herbert Walker, the scorer. Bright was a martinet: if he didn't like you, or if you had offended him in some way (which was not difficult), you got no treatment. He also appointed himself unofficial watchdog of the players' social activities. Once, in London, our party was distributed between two hotels, the Denmark and Snow's. In the Denmark, our masseur/timekeeper sat up until four o'clock one morning, then gleefully reported to the captain at breakfast, 'Booth, Lowson and Trueman had not come in by that time.'

Norman Yardley made enquiries, then summoned Bright and told him, 'You silly ass. You sat up until four a.m. in the Denmark and those three players were in bed at Snow's. I hope you enjoyed yourself.'

I once checked into my room in Portsmouth, looked out of the window and saw a submarine – the first I had ever seen – making its way out of the dockyard. I thought to myself, this is a pleasant room with a nice view. I'm going to enjoy my weekend here. I went out for a meal, came back and found Herbert Walker, asleep and snoring, in the middle of the only bed in the room.

'What's going on?' I demanded, shaking him awake.

He was cross at being awakened and told me, 'This is my bed. Yours is in the bathroom.' I found a board had been put in position over the top of the bath and made up into a bed, so the fast bowler spent the weekend on that while the masseur had a nice double bed to himself.

Walker was very much a typical Yorkshireman. When we travelled by coach he insisted on occupying the front seat, across from the driver, and would allow no one else to sit there ... until, that was, he was supposed to be navigating us to Southend. 'Not far to go,' he sang out, cheerfully. 'I've just seen a signpost: Southend – twelve miles.' We travelled for nearly an hour and then someone saw another signpost, which read: Southend – twenty-six miles. We changed the seating-plan after that.

Herbert used to keep a note of catches in his scorebook and, more particularly, dropped catches – or what he personally decreed to be missed chances. You might dive five or six yards and just get your fingertips to the ball – and it would go down in Herbert's book with a red mark to denote a miss. As such things determined whether or not the captain would approve your end-of-season bonus, Herbert made himself a bit unpopular at times. I must say, he didn't flinch, however, and carried on with his own methods and decisions, despite all entreaties. You can't change a Yorkshireman!

It was something of a surprise to me when Peter Howard Parfitt gave up county cricket when he was still only thirty-five and batting as well as ever, to move more than two hundred miles away from Middlesex, and his native Norfolk, and make his home in the Yorkshire Dales, five miles from me.

In fact he bought a small pub with semi derelict outbuildings, and within a few years he had transformed a hostelry of one and a half public rooms into a magnificent place with restaurant and conference room and a clientele which came from miles around. A bit of a go-getter, our Peter. However, he had not finished yet. He sold the pub when he felt he had gone as far as he could up that particular road, and launched a completely new career in corporate hospitality at Test match grounds, rugby internationals ... you name it, Parf has been there.

I was surprised, as I say, when he arrived in my part of the world – surprised and grateful. It has given me a cricket pal right on my own doorstep: we swop visits, have dinner, start talking – and it takes only a few minutes before *Wisden*, or some other cricket reference book, comes out and we are away down Memory Lane. Peter has always been a profound and astute cricket thinker and we are never short of a topic to discuss.

Peter was a mate, but not a specially close friend, in his playing days. His associates were his Middlesex team-mates, J. T. Murray and Fred Titmus, whom I also liked. I like to think that the cordial association of all four of us helped to bring about a distinct improvement in relations between Yorkshire and Middlesex.

Yorkshire before the war were certainly a good, efficient and successful team, but my word, did they not store up a lot of unpopularity for themselves? I once went for lunch with some friends to the Mumbles Hotel, near Swansea, in the 1950s and was told, 'You are the first Yorkshire cricketer to be allowed in here since before the war.' This startled me, but gradually I began to realise how much hostility and antipathy had been created in the pre-war years. Most of the umpires of the 1950s had been pre-war players, and there was some bitterness amongst Yorkshire teams that umpires 'never gave 'em nowt'. From almost every other county side we felt an attitude of deepest resentment, And nowhere was this more pointed than in Yorkshire v. Middlesex games. The post-war Yorkshire teams could not account for this at all, but I like to think that in the sixties and seventies some of us did a bit to put matters straight.

Parfitt was a good left-hand batsman who would have been outstanding in another era – such as the present one – but he had to compete for a place with players like Ted Dexter, Mike Smith, Geoff Pullar, Peter Richardson, Ken Barrington, Tom Graveney, Colin Cowdrey, Bob Barber and David Sheppard. He played in thirty-seven Tests without ever being able to feel he had an assured place.

Peter, as long as I've known him, has had a distinctive voice

– loud and penetrating – and it was often heard on the cricket field. With Titmus as bowler, Parfitt at slip and 'JT' behind the stumps, there was usually a fair amount of chat going on in the Middlesex ranks – and it was not always aimed at bringing ease and comfort to the batsman. Murray once told Parfitt, 'You have a stage whisper that Laurence Olivier would be proud of,' and certainly I've known Peter's voice to be clearly identifiable across three or four holes of a golf course.

He absolutely idolised Denis Compton and has a hundred stories about him; in fact Parf has an after-dinner repertoire which is said to consist of one half Compton and one half Trueman. This caused a little difficulty on one occasion when he was invited to address the annual dinner of the Association of Golf Writers, on the eve of the Open championship. The two principal guests were a couple of promising young golfers named Severiano Ballesteros and Bernhard Langer. Neither, at the time, was especially fluent in English, and I'm quite sure neither of them had ever heard of Denis Compton or Freddie Trueman.

I once had to give Peter a bollocking out in the middle at The Gabba, in Brisbane. He was heading for a hundred despite being placed at number seven in the batting order. Even A. C. Smith, in his first Test, had gone in ahead of him – what on earth was Ted Dexter thinking about? – and Parf had clearly decided his chances of reaching his ton with only the tail as partners were not very good. I told him, 'Calm down. I can bat a bit and I'll keep you company as long as I can. Don't chuck away the chance of a century against Australia.' He mustn't have trusted me, however, as he was out for 80, trying to hit Richie Benaud over the top. Still, he did score seven Test centuries and averaged over 40, and he held 564 catches in 387 matches, 42 of them in his 37 Tests.

Parfitt has always had a highly individual sense of humour. After rebuilding and re-establishing his Yorkshire pub, and adding an extensive car park, he then erected three flagpoles. He occasionally flew the flags of Yorkshire CCC and Middlesex

CCC from the two outside poles, while the middle one carried a banner of three horizontal stripes, the two outer ones of crimson and the middle one of gold.

Who 'grassed' on him, I don't know, but Parf received an exceedingly pompous letter from Jack Bailey, Secretary at that time of the MCC, demanding to know who had given him permission to display the colours of the Marylebone Cricket Club in some remote Yorkshire outpost!

Peter thought about this for a long time, then answered the letter. It was true, he said, that he flew the flag of the county for which he had played, and no one in Middlesex had objected. It was true that he flew the flag of the county in which he now lived, and there had been no objection from that quarter, either.

The third flag, he explained, was that of the constitutional monarchy of Spain, and while it was always pleasant to receive a letter from the headquarters of world cricket, he was curious to know why they were interested.

He did not hear again from NW8, but it was reported that Jack Bailey had been seen biting lumps out of his office carpet.

Parf, in his after-dinner speeches, enjoys telling of his first meeting with me. He came out to bat at Lord's as an enthusiastic and dashing young man of nineteen and encountered Frederick for the first time. Anxious to make a favourable impression, he tried to hook before he had given himself time to judge the pace of the pitch – and suffered severe damage to his handsome features. He was led away for repairs and returned three or four wickets later to continue his innings.

This, please bear in mind, is Peter's story, not mine, and he swears the following dialogue took place as he walked past me to take his place at the crease.

FST: 'Are you all right, son?'

PHP: 'Yes, Mr Trueman, thank you. I'm fine.'

FST (after a significant and threatening pause): 'I'm glad to hear it. They don't usually come back so quick after I've hit 'em.'

16

===

Umpires

I have known a lot of good umpires and some that were *very* good. I have also encountered a few who don't come into either category. Rarely, though, have I encountered an umpire who wasn't, one way or another, a character.

Almost the first one I can recall was Alec Skelding, a medium-fast bowler for Leicestershire from 1912 to 1929 and then an umpire for twenty-seven years. He did not retire until he was seventy-two, and was still giving a smile to players in his last year. Very little escaped Alec's sense of humour or his gift for the dramatic.

It was, I suppose, inevitable that when the first hat-trick of lbw victims fell to a bowler, the umpire standing at the bowler's end should be Alexander Skelding.

Try, if you can, to put yourself in his position. In only his second year on the first-class list, he found himself standing at Bramall Lane, Sheffield, when Yorkshire played Somerset. Horace Fisher, a slow left-arm bowler, appealed for an lbw decision and Alec, having satisfied himself that all the requirements had been met, replied confidently, 'That's out.'

Just over two minutes later, the new batsman having arrived and taken guard, Horace was asking the same question again.

Alec gave it a bit of thought before announcing to the world, 'And that's out as well.'

With another batsman hastily buckling on his pads, it wasn't too long before Skelding again heard the question he had dreaded: 'How's that?' His brain must have been in a turmoil – there had never before been a hat-trick of lbw victims. Did he perhaps consider this as bowler and fieldsmen looked at him with something more than the usual degree of expectancy?

Alec took a deep breath, raised his eyes to the heavens and stepped into the pages of cricketing history with the immortal words: 'As God is my judge, that's out as well.'

His humour had a laconic, almost sly quality. I was talking to him once at Northampton just after I had made my first hundred, when he mentioned, 'I once got a hundred, you know.'

Surprised (because Alec's first-class average when he retired was 6.76), I replied, 'Did you really?'

'Aye,' said he. 'I started in April and I finished in September. But I did make a hundred runs.'

Alec could be helpful on the field. One day when I couldn't get everything right, but couldn't decide what I was doing wrong, I said to him at the end of an over, 'I don't know what's wrong with me today. Will you have a look at me from square-leg when you get a chance, and see if you can tell me what the trouble is?'

'Certainly,' said Alec, and he did.

Brian Statham was once bowling, with Bill Copson, the old Derbyshire fast bowler, standing as umpire at his end and things were not going too well. Brian looked ruefully at the ball, which had seen quite a bit of service in that innings, and remarked conversationally to Bill, 'This seam's as flat as a fart.'

The umpire responded, 'Well —ing well lift it, then. That's what I used to do.' It was the sort of comment which wouldn't, I suppose, go down too well in Pakistan these days.

We claim in England that our umpires are the best in the world, because the great majority are former players – and I think that's right. Our modern players ought to reflect on how lucky they are: English umpires know the game from the inside. They have been there. They can be relied upon to know the problems.

It is a different matter in overseas countries, particularly in the West Indies and (usually for quite different reasons) Australia. I have seen West Indian umpires who were terrified of the crowd if they gave an unpopular decision. I remember a chap called Perry Burke, standing in Jamaica, giving an 'out' decision against J. K. Holt Jnr . . . and his wife and kids were beaten up at a railway station. Not surprisingly, we didn't get many decisions in our favour after that.

There was an umpire called Kippins officiating on the 1959–60 tour of the West Indies who wouldn't give us a thing, and I remember someone asking him if one decision hadn't been very close. He replied, 'I couldn't give it because I couldn't see any stumps. He was covering the lot.'

Another one, called Jordan, stood in Barbados during that series, and when he was told, 'The only two people I know who take the field in dark glasses are you and the Duke of Edinburgh,' he replied, 'Thank you.' He thought it was a compliment.

In Trinidad every lbw appeal got the same answer: 'Too high.' Then Brian Statham hit a batsman very low on the pad and straight in front, but the umpire said, 'Not out.'

At the end of the over, Geoff Pullar, keeping his face straight, asked him, 'I suppose that was going *under* the stumps?'

He was told, 'Yes.'

Once, at Sabina Park, Kingston, I had been bowling for hours, it seemed, up the hill, hitting the pads from time to time and always getting the same reply: 'Not out.' Eventually my disillusionment must have shown, and Peter May, the captain, walked across and put an arm around my shoulders. 'Come on, Freddie,' he said. 'You're bowling well and it's been a great effort. Don't let them get you down. England expects, you know.'

'England expects,' I echoed. 'Is that why they call it the *mother* country?' It was said with some bitterness but at least the captain saw the joke.

On the other hand, I must say that we were so impressed by the fair and impartial umpiring of Lee Kow in Trinidad on the 1959–60 tour that the manager asked if he could be appointed to stand in the next Test in Jamaica. I believe that was the first time it had been done. It's good to see that in more recent years Steve Bucknor has become internationally recognised as one of the outstanding umpires in the world.

The Australians have what might be described as a more cynical approach to things – at least that was my experience on the 1958–9 tour when our batsmen were given no protection at all against the 'suspect' deliveries of Ian Meckiff, Gordon Rorke and Keith Slater. I vividly remember one conversation in which one or two of us drew attention to Slater's action and an Aussie official grinned, 'Well, at least he's chucking *straight*, isn't he, mate?'

Even the great Don Bradman once, unwittingly, gave a bit of substance to our complaints about Australian umpiring. He was talking to Brian Johnston and myself about an umpire called Mel McInnes, and we were complaining about his lack of 'feel' for the game. 'Oh, come on,' said The Don. 'He was a good player himself . . . until his eyesight went.' There was a moment's silence; we all looked at each other. Sir Donald, realising the implication of what he had said, roared with laughter, and we joined in.

One of the great umpiring remarks of all time must be that of Arthur Jepson, formerly of Notts, who was standing at Old Trafford during that celebrated limited-overs match against Gloucestershire which went on until a few seconds before nine p.m.

It was late in the day when Jackie Bond, the Lancashire captain, came in to bat. The lights were on in the pavilion and in Warwick Road station; the moon and stars were clearly visible in the night sky. Bond looked at Jepson and asked, 'What are we doing, playing in this light?'

'Jeppo' replied, tartly, 'What about the light?'

'Well, it's pretty dark, isn't it?' retorted Jackie, staunchly.

What do you reckon then, Skippy?....
Do you think he was out?....
You don't think he was, eh?....

'What's that up there?' questioned Jepson, gazing up at the sky.

Bond responded, 'Well, that's what I mean – it's the moon, isn't it?'

Jepson returned, 'And how far away is *that*?'

Bond thought for a minute, and replied 'It's about two hundred and sixty thousand miles, isn't it?'

Jepson ended the conversation with, 'Then how bloody far do you want to see?'

I think John Arlott's favourite umpiring story concerned a last-wicket partnership between 'Lofty' Herman, Hampshire's number eleven batsman, and his captain Lord Tennyson, during the 1930s. The couple needed to hold out for a fair length of time to save the game, and Lord Tennyson plainly had very little faith in his partner's ability to do so.

'If the chance comes, appeal against the light,' he instructed his partner who, gazing up through bright sunlight to a blue sky, offered the view that such a request might not be received with too much sympathy. 'Just do your best,' was how the captain rounded off the conversation.

A few minutes later, as Lord Tennyson called his partner for a single, Lofty had a moment of magnificent inspiration. He ignored the call, peered intently down the pitch, and responded, 'I hear you, my lord, but I cannot see you.'

John also recalled one of those mix-ups which sometimes occur when a batsman is using a runner. He swore it was absolutely true that the injured batsman (who must have made a sharp recovery), his partner *and* the runner, went up and down the pitch, three abreast, three times, variously shouting, 'Yes,' 'No,' and 'Wait,' before the bails were removed. Even then no decision could be given, because both umpires, as well as the fieldsmen, were rolling about on the ground, laughing.

Jim Laker had one great memory of touring India with a Commonwealth XI just after the war and playing against one of the princely states, Patiala. George Tribe, that splendid Australian left-arm purveyor of 'funny stuff', was bowling at the end where the umpire standing was a senior member of the maharajah's staff. 'Not out,' he responded stoically to every appeal. George, who was repeatedly beating the bat and rapping the pads, became increasingly agitated, but when the maharajah himself came in to bat, the 'Not outs' became even more frequent and correspondingly more emphatic.

'Finally,' said Jim, 'and I've never seen anything like it in all my life, George grabbed the little umpire by his shirt front and demanded, "Have another look, you silly bugger."'

'The umpire, visibly shaken, peered down the pitch and responded, "Oh my goodness, you are right, Mr Tribe. Your Serene Highness – I very much regret that you are *not in*."'

My old mate and new-ball partner of the 1960s, Tony Nicholson, had an attitude towards umpires which perhaps might best be described as ambivalent. There was no malice in Tony – I don't think he ever actively disliked anyone in his life – but he did believe with quite passionate sincerity in the righteousness of every appeal he ever addressed to an umpire. He was utterly convinced that his cause was just. There have been louder appealers; there have been bowlers who invested their cries of 'How's that?' with greater histrionic detail. But never has there been a man who was more convinced that his shout was justified.

The man we knew as 'Nick' kept a mental league table of those umpires who had rejected his appeals, and the number of rejections by each one of them. He did not make his findings public, though it has to be said that he did, from time to time, 'think aloud' about the injustices a cruel officialdom inflicted upon him.

These league tables might have remained forever undetected if it had not been for Tommy Spencer. Tommy had played for Kent before and for one season after the Second World War, and became an umpire in 1950. He remained on the first-class list for thirty years (including seventeen Tests), so he knew his stuff. Nick, however, believed firmly that Tommy had some personal grudge against him. It was during a game at Bramall

Lane that Nick appealed for lbw and gazed, in massive disbelief, as Mr Spencer replied, 'Not out.' In circumstances like this, Tony used to adopt what we called his 'teapot' stance. He would stand for a long moment of silent incomprehension with his right hand on his hip, but on that day in Sheffield he was moved to break his silence.

'That's twenty-bloody-seven,' he lamented to no one in particular.

Someone – it might have been Jimmy Binks, our wicket-keeper – asked, curiously, 'What's up, Nick?' and then all was revealed.

'Twenty-bloody-seven times he's turned me down,' said A. G. Nicholson. 'And that's only *this* season.'

Cecil George Pepper, the big-hitting Australian all-rounder (who was a renowned league professional and whose straight six over the boarding-houses into Trafalgar Square at Scarborough was the biggest hit most people on the ground have ever seen) was an umpire in England from 1964 to 1979. He was a genial soul who liked nothing better than to join in whatever conversation was taking place on the field.

In the early seventies Pepper was standing at Park Avenue, Bradford, with Don Oslear, who was a new umpire, and, significantly, one who had not played first-class cricket. The match was Yorkshire v. Leicestershire and, to the surprise of no one except, apparently, Oslear, a snarling match broke out between Geoffrey Boycott, opening for Yorkshire, and Ken Higgs, veteran of many a Roses match for Lancashire, and now recruited by Leicestershire after three years of 'retirement'. There was, you might say, no love lost between batsman and bowler, as the former played and missed and the latter expressed his considered opinion that the batsman had been a trifle fortunate. The adjective spawny was frequently used, and doubts were cast on parentage.

The exchanges became increasingly colourful but no one took much notice beyond grinning – except Mr Oslear, who had plainly never heard anything like it in his career. After one particularly lurid passage he felt it necessary to ask the fielding captain to restrain the comments of his bowler. The Leicestershire captain just happened to be Raymond Illingworth, no stranger to Roses warfare himself. Raymond pondered the strange request which had just been addressed to him, then, at the end of the over, sauntered across to the other umpire, Pepper, with a suggestion.

'I think you'd better tell your mate,' Raymond said, 'to keep out of that bit of bother. It's a private matter and has nowt to do with him.' 'Pep' was only too happy to oblige.

Pepper, I used to think, enjoyed most the occasions when he was umpiring and his fellow Australian, Bill Alley, was playing. This brought together two of the greatest 'talkers' of their day. Later, as an umpire, Bill never stopped talking! 'Pep' rarely got the better of Alley. Once, at Aclam Park, Middlesbrough, Pepper walked all the way to the boundary edge, between overs, and asked a spectator to go out and buy a packet of birdseed. When the spectator returned with the packet, to Pepper's surprise, he walked over to the great Somerset all-rounder and handed him – without a word, and better than any punchline – the packet of Trill.

Alley himself became a first-class umpire, and stood in Tests, after retiring as a player – and what a player he was. After a three-year career with New South Wales he came to play league cricket in Lancashire, broke one record after another, and did not enter county cricket over here until 1957, when he was thirty-eight. All the same, he reached 1,000 runs ten times, scored 3,019 runs in 1961 and did the double the following year. A wonderful cricketer, Bill Alley.

No collection of umpiring stories would be complete without some mention of Harold Dennis Bird, known the world over as 'Dickie', who retired from Test umpiring in 1996. Everyone knows Dickie, the archetypal Yorkshireman, the eternal pessimist, the man who has been beset by misfortune – real or imagined – throughout his cricketing life. For twenty-five years, rain has scanned the county fixture lists for games where

it is known Dickie will be standing, and if rain could not be present in person it has passed on the relevant information to its colleague, bad light. *Off* the field, similar misfortunes have tracked Dickie down relentlessly.

Just two or three years ago Dickie joined Ian Botham and myself in a series of speaking engagements in South Africa, and headwinds delayed our flight into Johannesburg considerably. John Edrich was waiting to meet us, and as a British Airways official, he was able to 'hold' our connecting flight to Durban for a time. We were whisked through Customs and Immigration, but before we could board the waiting plane for Durban we had to pass once again through a security check. Ian and I passed through without a problem and so did our wives, Kathy and Veronica. When it came to Dickie's turn, however, 'ping' went the alarm.

'No problem,' said the officials. 'Let's try it again.'

Once more Dickie ran the gauntlet of metal-detectors and once more there was the warning 'ping'.

Dickie turned out his pockets and took off his belt – still the detector didn't like him. On the plane, a couple of hundred perspiring South Africans began to get a bit restive. Why was the flight being delayed? At the security check, Dickie was sweating, too. The temperature was eighty-six degrees and, for some reason I have never understood, Dickie was wearing in addition to his blazer, a red sweater. There was nothing for it but to take him off to a private room and subject him to a strip search. While Edrich valiantly fought off all attempts to get the plane to take off for Durban, Dickie – down to the buff – was examined for concealed grenades and handguns. Nothing was found.

He re-dressed, now reduced to a state of gibbering apoplexy, and then at last, the cause of the 'pings' was discovered: a half-crown, which had slipped into the torn lining of Dickie's blazer. Half-crowns had been out of circulation for how long? Twenty years or so? Oh yes – Dickie was a good Yorkshireman. The only mystery was why the lost half-crown had remained missing for so long. Surely he had looked for it himself?

It was during that trip to South Africa that Dickie revealed his experience with the Giant Parrot. Dickie started to tell the tale with only the Bothams, the Truemans and Fran Cotton, the rugby player as his audience, in a hotel lounge. He completed it with a crowd of several hundred gathered round, and, at the end, he received a magnificent round of applause.

At the end of the previous cricket season, Dickie had received an invitation to act as a judge at a caged-bird show to be staged at the National Exhibition Centre in Birmingham. His protestations that he 'knew nowt about birds' were brushed aside. He just had to turn up at the NEC. There would be no problems caused by his lack of ornithological expertise, but would he please bring his umpiring cap and boots. A white coat would be provided.

This last piece of information should have started the alarm bells ringing, but Dickie – as I say, a good Yorkshireman – was more interested in the last line of the correspondence: there would, of course, be a fee for his services as a judge.

So off he went to Birmingham, put on the white coat and his umpiring cap and cricket boots . . . and was told that he would be the judge of the talking birds section.

Dickie was led into the vastness of the NEC, packed with warm-blooded, egg-laying, feathered vertebrates of the class Aves and, in almost equal numbers, a horde of newspaper photographers. Those of you who have had contact with press cameramen will know that they never want to take the obvious picture – for the perfectly sound reason that everyone else will have that one. Every newspaper photographer wants something different, and the dafter the difference, the better pleased they are. However, on this occasion, there was an unusual degree of unanimity amongst the paparazzi. They all wanted a shot of Dickie in conversation with the largest bird in the section, a parrot which was, according to Dickie, 'bloody enoooormous'.

Dickie's duties were relatively straightforward. He had simply to adjudicate on which bird was, in the opinion of Mr Bird, international arbiter, the best talker. So, dutifully and industriously, he walked up and down the serried ranks of budgerigars, toucans, mynahs and macaws, chatting happily away.

All the birds responded to greater or lesser degree – except the Giant Parrot, the principal object of the photographers' immediate attention, which refused even to open its eyes. It reacted only once, when one particularly enterprising cameraman lifted it (not without difficulty) from its perch and placed it on Dickie's head. The bird promptly, copiously and comprehensively, relieved itself.

Dickie's response – piteously regaled to his audience in South Africa – was anguished: 'Ee, it were awful. It ran all over me cap and started dripping down me face.'

Something had to give – and it was the parrot. After a good quarter of an hour of pleading and coaxing ('Come on, then, Sunshine . . . I want you to say summat . . . say owt tha' likes . . . be a good lad, come on . . .') the Giant Parrot at last relented.

Gradually the hooded eyes opened . . . wide. It subjected Dickie, the world's best-known umpire, to a baleful stare and finally delivered its verdict.

Slowly, but quite clearly and distinctly, it uttered one word: 'Bollocks', and promptly closed its eyes again.

17

My Father

Alan Trueman is *exactly* the sort of chap you would expect to find walking around Scotch Springs, because he was my father . . . the father I loved and respected and who gave me standards on which I have based my life.

He taught me to respect authority when it was soundly based and intelligent in its application, but never to accept bullying authority for its own sake. He taught me never to suffer fools gladly, and to judge a man on what he did and said, not merely on what he was.

Together with my brother and my sister, I went to church three times on Sunday – morning service, Sunday School and evensong – and to this day I regularly attend Sunday matins at the lovely old parish church at Bolton Priory in one of the most spectacularly beautiful parts of Wharfedale.

We walked a mile and a half to school five days a week, and at the end of the day we walked back. It was, thank God, safe for children to walk about unescorted in the 1930s.

I learned at a very early age to polish my shoes before going to bed at night, so that they shone when I went out in the morning, and I follow the habit religiously sixty-five years later. One of the things I most detest is to see a man with dirty shoes.

It was a warm, loving and close-knit family unit, and just how much that means to a child's happiness and security was something I was only able to appreciate fully in the years ahead. All I knew at the time was that I felt comfortable and grateful for the good things in life. We children were encouraged to feel we were making a contribution. We picked peas and lifted potatoes, topped and tailed mangolds. On a Friday night we got free potatoes to take home, so that was the time to find the biggest bucket available.

My mother baked half a dozen loaves of bread a day, and always I remember the smell of fresh baking as one of those things which enrich one's childhood recollections. Seasonally, we picked wild raspberries and blackberries to provide more richness and variety to the family table. We kept hens and pigs, so there were always fresh eggs and, twice a year, the mouthwatering fare of roast pork.

Those were days when families like ours – and there were so many of them around the country – created their own entertainment, and found it all the more enjoyable for that. Cricket began with three stumps chalked on a wall and graduated to a propped-up dustbin lid. My father played with us, gently encouraging and giving us elementary coaching in the basics. He was a slow left-arm bowler and got many mentions in the local newspapers. Later I learned that my grandfather, Albert, had had an opportunity to go to the Yorkshire nets but, with native canniness had costed the exercise and found he could make more money buying and selling horses, so cricket remained, to him, a pastime.

By the time I was ten, my father was spending hours coaching and encouraging me and, looking back, I marvel that he found the time. He had a full-time job, ran two allotments to grow our fresh vegetables, looked after the hens and pigs, roughly but kindly tutoring his children, and yet he still managed to play his cricket at the weekends and to coach his sons. Twice a year my father played against Worksop, where Ken Farnes, the England opening bowler, was a master at the college. I quite vividly remember walking down the main street of Worksop in

1939, holding my father's hand on one side and Ken Farnes' on the other.

Something must have rubbed off on me, because by the time I was in my mid-teens I was able to generate a remarkable amount of pace, and, playing for Roche Abbey, I had taken thirty or forty wickets for about three runs apiece. My father wrote to Cyril Turner, the former Yorkshire all-rounder, who had become coach at Sheffield United CC, and he came to see me in action. That's how it all began to happen.

Some of the lessons you learn as a child remain with you throughout your life. The influence my father exerted has stayed with me, and I shall be grateful for it as long as I live. He nurtured me through a happy childhood; he saw me safely on my way to a career in cricket; he accompanied me on my first trip to the Yorkshire nets; he saw me take my first Test wicket, and there was time for him to see me take my three hundredth.

I can still see him sitting in his chair on the evening of the day I was awarded my Yorkshire cap . . . wrapped in a cocoon of sheer happiness. I don't think people today can appreciate what a call-up by Yorkshire meant to a youngster of forty and fifty years ago, or what it meant to a youngster's parents. He sat, that evening, mulling over the wonder of it all. His lad had been awarded a Yorkshire cap. The boy was now on a par with Hirst and Rhodes, with Sutcliffe and Hutton, at least in terms of what kept the sun out of our eyes! I gave that cap to my father. It literally went to the grave with him . . . in his coffin.

I am so very grateful that he was able to see some of what came later. I used to tell him of the people I had met and the conversations I had had, and his eyes used to fill with tears. I was talking about men who, in my father's life, were the stuff of history.

He never at any time bullied, but he knew, instinctively, how to encourage. He had not hesitated, once he thought I might be good enough, to write to other, higher authorities on my behalf. I hope I repaid my father, just a little, for all he gave to me.

Epilogue

In conclusion, perhaps I may offer a few thoughts on the modern game. My exasperated cry of 'I don't know what's going off out there' has been seized on, delightedly, by the impressionists (and by some critics who never *will* know what is happening out in the middle), but I am quite honestly lost for words on occasions. To see bowlers consistently bowling the wrong line (that is if they are bowling any discernible line at all) is quite unbelievable. I do not often feel sympathy for Michael Atherton's captaincy but I certainly felt it when he was criticised for his field-placing during that last-wicket partnership in Auckland in 1997 which saved the Test for New Zealand. Just how can any captain set a field for bowlers who can't bowl on one side of the pitch?

Any specific criticism of individual players on that winter tour which exposed so many shortcomings would be obviously fraught with danger, since these thoughts are being recorded *after* that tour but *before* the major part of the 1997 summer series. Nevertheless, I cannot resist the temptation to voice a few personal views.

Michael Atherton, for all his natural ability as a batsman, struck a spell of poor form and yet was allowed a whole series of Tests and one-day internationals in which to play himself back into nick, something I cannot remember happening too often in the past. Graeme Hick is likely to become the youngest man in history to score a hundred hundreds, and is obviously a player of immense ability, yet after a series of low Test scores he was discarded. Will he ever be recalled?

When I first saw Graham Thorpe I thought straightaway that he was destined to be a Test-class batsman. I have been disappointed to see him get out too many times when apparently well set, so it was all the more pleasing to see him come good at Edgbaston in the First Test of 1997. He has outstanding class.

John Crawley has the natural ability to become the best batsman in the side and he should certainly be batting at number three of four, not lower down the order.

Robert Croft was the 'find' of the 1996–7 winter tour. Why on earth has it taken so long for his talent to be recognised? Perhaps for the same reason that his mentor, Don Shepherd, took over 2,200 wickets in his first-class career and was never selected for a Test.

Andrew Caddick looks to me to be the best new-ball bowler in the country, but I think he would do even better if he pitched the ball just a little further up.

Darren Gough, for all his success at Edgbaston (June 1997) will never be a *fast* bowler as long as he lives, not with *that* action! He should concentrate on what he does best as a fast-medium seamer. He has a good yorker and a decent slower ball, but when he tries to bowl fast I worry about the legality of his delivery.

Dominic Cork is the sort of bowler England has always produced – a good fast-medium – but if conditions do not help swing he has a lot to learn. Please, though, could we have less of the histrionics when he takes a wicket? One would think he had never claimed a victim before – his antics are like someone auditioning for the Royal Shakespeare Company.

That said, it was good to see England start the summer of

1997 so successfully, even though I must say I was astonished that Australia keeled over in the First Test. Australians do not normally give in so easily so I was not in the least surprised by the fightback which came within weeks and was completed on the fourth day of the Trent Bridge Test.

That day, 10 August, perhaps illustrated as well as any other the difference between the sides in general and in detail. In the earlier half of the day England, on paper, were still in with a shout but a century partnership by Healy and Ponting changed the picture and made the England attack, not for the first time, look pretty ordinary. So England were left to make 451 and I can't think of anyone who might have expected them to do it. Even so, a total of 186 all out was, to say the least, a pretty poor apology for a fight.

It was an eight-over spell by Jason Gillespie which just about summed it all up – 8–0–65–3. All right, he was given an attacking field so there were bound to be gaps but eight an over from a side batting with its back to the wall suggests something a bit more than that. Gillespie's line was not good and it was certainly not consistent but he picked up the wickets of Hussain, Crawley and Adam Hollioake because of what I can only describe as some pretty sloppy undisciplined batting, and the match was as good as over. With showers forecast for the following day, Mark Taylor claimed the extra half-hour and the tail was unable to give Thorpe the support he needed to take the match into the final day.

It was not the sort of performance I would associate with most of the England teams I played with, either in batting or bowling. And it was no use blaming the selectors. As far as I could see, there were not too many alternatives around to the men who had been beaten at Old Trafford, Headingley and Trent Bridge.

Finally, as promised, the thoughts of Peter Parfitt on what we both see as the mistakes of the past thirty or forty years, and our suggestions on how things can be put right. Parf's words will find support from the overwhelming majority of players of the recent past at Test and county level, men whose thinking on the game is reasoned, reasonable and relevant. If English cricket is going to have respectability and credibility restored I most earnestly hope that Lord McLaurin and his Board will heed Parf's advice:

> I think before going into specifics it is important to say that modern players resent what they see as the suggestion by those of my generation that present-day cricketers can't play at all. That simply isn't true. God doesn't stop bestowing talent upon one generation in the way that He gave it to the previous one. That is a nonsense. No one can say that Gavaskar couldn't play, that Barry Richards couldn't play and that Tendulkar is not a player of immense ability. But if you haven't got the *system* right, then the ability and talent doesn't develop.
>
> Somebody told me not long ago that we have as many seventeen-year-olds playing cricket in this country today as there has ever been. So why do they not filter through? I believe that parents today – and indeed, the youngsters themselves – are extremely qualification-conscious. They have been told, and they believe, that there is a possibility they might never find employment. Cricket, in the past, has never been a generously paid occupation and I do believe children are saying to themselves, 'Hold on a minute. We have a question of priorities here. There are alternatives open to me. Which do I take?'
>
> Another point to bear in mind is that forty years ago England was a relatively labour-intensive nation. There were the mines and the steel industry, and the story was that if Derbyshire or Nottinghamshire, and to some extent Yorkshire and Lancashire, wanted a fast bowler they went and whistled down the nearest mine-shaft; a young man would appear who could bowl forty overs over the weekend and return to work at seven o'clock on Monday morning, none the worse for his recreational exercise. It was also true of Warwickshire and the Black Country's steelworks in relation to bowlers in the Birmingham League. That just isn't happening today, and contributes to the regularity with which our modern youngsters, especially the fast bowlers, break down so frequently.

Also, it has to be understood and accepted that the 'younger' cricketing nations, like Pakistan, Sri Lanka and – remarkably – Zimbabwe, have improved quickly and dynamically. You simply cannot escape that; you cannot ignore it. There is absolutely no comparison between the Pakistan teams I played against, and men like Wasim Akram and Waqar Younis.

More specifically, over the past forty years (i.e. since I started playing) a number of decisions have been made which did not, perhaps, have an immediate impact; however, the people who made those decisions did not appreciate how profound an effect they were to have in the long term.

(1) The old no-ball rule (judged on the position of the bowler's *back* foot) encouraged him to bowl from close to the wicket so that in some cases the hand holding the ball actually brushed the stumps on occasion. That developed the classic, side-on action, and enabled a bowler to deliver the outswinger from the most effective position and angle. More than that, it was a natural progression that having delivered the ball, the bowler's momentum carried him *away* from the pitch. The front-foot rule, on the other hand, has encouraged bowling from wide of the crease with a chest-on action which takes the bowler, on his follow-through, on a route which goes on to the pitch and, inevitably, damages it.

It is worth mentioning at this point that all the great finger-spinners of, say, the last fifty years, started off as 'little' medium-pace bowlers ... men like Tom Goddard, Raymond Illingworth, Don Shepherd, Bob Appleyard, Fred Titmus and, possibly the greatest of them all, Jim Laker. They all started their careers as medium-pacers and they all bowled with classic side-on actions.

Now let us take the additional point that we have never been a nation which produced *great* fast bowlers, although we had Larwood, Trueman and the 'blaster' in Tyson – who lasted barely four seasons – and, of the later generation, John Snow. We *have*, however, been a great nation of fast-medium swing and seam bowlers: Maurice Tate, George Geary, Reg Perks, Alec Bedser, Cliff Gladwin, Trevor Bailey ... and that's naming only a few. We have always produced that type in abundance and they have often been very successful abroad. Their success was, in large measure, due to that classic side-on action, which, in turn, was encouraged by the back-foot no-ball rule.

On the other hand, the 'new' rule (changed more than thirty years ago), using the position of the *front* foot, does encourage the wide-of-the-crease bowler and the open-chesters, and therefore favours the physical attributes and characteristics of the Afro-Caribbean bowler. It does the English-type bowler no favours at all. Therefore that change in the Laws, enacted around 1963 or 1964, has had a significant effect which was not foreseen at the time it was introduced, but which has developed alarmingly over a period of years.

(2) The change in the lbw rule has, in turn, had a profound effect upon certain important aspects of batsmanship. There was the stupid 'intent' definition (well intentioned, no doubt, in the first place, to discourage the padding-off, without offering a stroke, of balls pitched outside the off-stump) but its effect has been to encourage wide-of-the-crease lines of attack, and that, in turn, has promoted a lot of technically 'loose' batting, and a lot of needless bat-waving outside the off-stump. It has tended to make batsmen more inclined to go for off-side strokes rather than develop a wider repertoire of shots all round the ground. If you go back to the even older lbw rule, changed in the 1930s, you couldn't be out if the ball pitched outside the line of the off-stump. There was a lot to commend that, from a batting point of view, at any rate! It positively encouraged batsmen to play back, and it is self-evident that there are more strokes available to a batsman on the back foot than to one on the front foot. A great back-foot player is far more exciting to watch than a great front-foot player.

(3) I have to say that there is too much one-day cricket. The whole emphasis in limited-overs games is on containment, rather than dismissing batsmen, and over a period of time, bowlers lose the ability and skill to get batsmen out. This might sound silly but it did happen: 1971, Middlesex v. Yorkshire at Lord's in a Sunday League game, and we decided that if we could keep Geoffrey Boycott at the crease for forty overs we would win the match! How absurd it sounds even to discuss such a possibility in a cricket match, let alone put it into practice, but that was

our thinking about that game as a whole. It is the inevitable consequence of a game in which the emphasis is on containment rather than bowling the other side out.

The modern player complains that he 'plays too much cricket'. I believe we play too much of the wrong sort of cricket and not enough of the right sort. In 1961 I played in twenty-eight three-day county championship matches, and against both universities, against the Australian tourists and in three matches at the Scarborough Festival. That's 102 days of cricket. I probably played in half a dozen one-day benefit matches as well. There was no discussion in our dressing-room about playing too much cricket. It simply was not a topic which came up.

I am very reluctant to accept the modern view that too much cricket is played. What I certainly do accept is that there is too much charging about the motorways, too much driving two hundred miles to play a one-day match and then rushing two hundred miles back. We didn't have any of that, and therefore we had a considerable advantage over the modern player. Every Tuesday and Friday night we chucked our gear into the boot of the car and moved on from one county match to the next. It wasn't all that easy because this was in the days before motorways and we often arrived at hotels at two and three o'clock in the morning with a new game starting at eleven or eleven thirty a.m. Equally, it was before the days of motorway traffic jams and IRA bomb scares!

There was often an extra advantage to be gained, however. Somewhere on our way to the next port of call we would meet another county side heading in the opposite direction, and, over a shandy or a meal, we would have a chat with friends and rivals. This brings me to another important point which, in my view, is largely missing from the modern cricket scene.

There doesn't seem to be time, these days, for the modern practitioner to sit down for an hour or two to *talk* cricket. It gave me, in my earliest days with Middlesex, what I consider to be an advantage over modern players. Apart from having figures in the dressing-room like Denis Compton, Bill Edrich, Jack Young and Jack Robertson, old players used to drop in . . . men like Patsy Hendren, Jack Hearne, Harry Lee, Len Muncer and Harry Sharp.

To sit on the grass at the Nursery End and have half an hour to talk to some of them was, in my view, absolutely invaluable. I have never wavered in that view and I never shall.

(4) We now have the four-day game and I am not entirely convinced about its value. To begin with, roughly the same number of overs are being bowled in four days as we used to bowl in three, which brings me to what I consider to be the greatest 'crime' in modern cricket.

All over the world it seems to have been accepted that fifteen overs an hour is all that is required. Today's players claim that they are much fitter than we were forty years ago, and I do not for a minute dispute that. Why, then, can they not bowl twenty overs an hour, as used to be the norm for the less-fit cricketers of yesterday?

In 1930, Bradman scored 304 in a day at Headingley and England bowled 139 overs in that day. In 1946, in Alec Bedser's first Test match, England completed their first post-war win in time for a leisurely lunch on the third day ... and a total of 348.5 overs had been bowled. I think that is *very* relevant. I was talking to Alec Bedser about this recently and he mentioned that after bowling through the 1954 season in England he went on the winter tour to Australia, and by 1 July the following year he had bowled 3,000 overs in just over fourteen months of first-class cricket – and he didn't break down. There were other bowlers doing nearly as much work as that, and they didn't break down, either.

I find it difficult to understand why a bowler in county cricket today is fined if he doesn't maintain eighteen overs an hour, and yet two days later the same bowler is permitted to bowl fifteen overs an hour in a Test match. Another aspect of increasing the over-rate is that you get the slower bowlers involved and add an extra dimension to the cricket.

Increasing the rate *can* be done. Jack Simmons, formerly of Lancashire, told me only the other day of an occasion when his side needed to increase the over-rate late one afternoon and he and David Lloyd bowled thirty-five overs in an hour! I wonder if the present England coach remembers it?

No one has exploited the slowing down of the over-rate more

cynically than the West Indies, and they have simply been allowed to get away with it. At times their bowling rate has dropped as low as ten overs an hour. Consider, if you will, the implications of this. Ten overs an hour means that at one end Curtley Ambrose, Courtney Walsh, Ian Bishop or whoever, is bowling *five* overs in an hour. That translates as one delivery every two minutes. Just how much dynamic and explosive quality can a fast bowler invest in one ball every two minutes?

Yet when the matter has been raised at ICC meetings the West Indies representatives have said, innocently, 'But we are still winning our matches when we are bowling at that rate.' Of course they are, because they are playing to their own set of rules! Other countries have to bowl at a higher over-rate to enable the West Indies to pile up the totals they do amass.

Will someone explain to me why Bob Willis and Graham Gooch – one recent England captain, the other even more recent – went to a TCCB meeting in 1996 and (I have this on very good authority) voted against increasing the required over-rate?

(5) Uncovered wickets is an issue, and a very important one. It is an absolute nonsense for the game's administrators to say this is not an option. It most certainly *is* an option, and one that has got to be pursued. There is so much evidence that we were a better bowling side on uncovered pitches and, technically, a better batting side, that it cannot be ignored. Let me illustrate with a little story.

In 1964–5 we were looking at the pitch in Durban before the First Test, and it was an absolute 'road', a cart-track. The great Walter Hammond said (as he was to say something similar to Fred Trueman on another occasion), 'What you have got to appreciate is that we [England] are the best players on the worst wickets in the world. And on every tour, you very rarely escape at some time a poor pitch.'

We listened to what Hammond said. We played the extra spinner, won the match by an innings and the series 1–0.

More than anything else, it was uncovered wickets which encouraged finger-spinners (like Laker, Titmus, Illingworth and others) to *experiment*, mixing seamers with their spinners and applying other variations. I was talking about this to Alec Bedser at Denis Compton's funeral in 1997, and he showed me the middle knuckle of his right hand. It was twice the size of the one on his left hand, the legacy of developing the leg-cutter – and what a magnificent bowler that made Bedser!

Robert Croft was indeed the 'find' of the 1996–7 tour, and it was certainly a revelation to see this young man bowling with a classic action and achieving entirely deserved success. I am forced to add, however, that thirty or forty years ago there were seventeen or more like him playing in first-class cricket – possibly not as good as Croft, but certainly possessing most of his characteristics and virtues. Every county had at least one of his kind, and we have to ask why they are not around any more.

(6) I don't think the debate on modern English cricket can be engaged without reference to the overseas player. The effect of overseas recruitment has clearly been considerable. There are, I think, two aspects of this, one being the enhancement of a county's performances, and I don't think there is much doubt that in some cases an overseas player has made his county into a better side (e.g. Phil Simmons, with Leicestershire in 1996, Desmond Haynes and Wayne Daniel with Middlesex). However, you have to weigh this against their contribution to English cricket, and in my view this has been negligible. It is difficult to see how their presence has improved English cricket in any material respect. At the same time, they have also been a very substantial drain on the financial resources of county clubs ... resources which could have been devoted to bringing on our own young players. That is certainly a long-term policy rather than an immediate solution, but it is vitally necessary for the improvement of our domestic game.

Some years ago John Major, the then Prime Minister, talked of 'getting back to basics', and I think that applies as much to cricket as to anything else. We have to look at areas where we were good, ask why those virtues were lost, and decide what we can do about it. I don't believe radical changes to the format of the game are the answer.

Lord McLaurin said he would like to see closer links between club cricket and the county game. That could be a good thing. Obviously if you improve the standard of club cricket you are going to improve the recruiting possibilities for the counties.

Splitting the county championship into two halves, however, can only be seen as *reducing* the number of good players in the game, and I cannot see how that can possibly improve standards.

There is talk of needing an academy for young cricketers, and this is usually with the Australian system in mind. What has to be borne in mind is that the population of Australia is about the size of the population of Greater London. What is needed is not one academy but several – almost one in every county. If we achieve that, then it is absolutely vital that we make use of the skills of older players. The Australians certainly do, and look at the results it has produced. I don't necessarily mean former players should be engaged in day-to-day coaching, but if they were simply around to talk to youngsters, to pass on the benefits of their experience, it would be of immeasurable help. I cannot emphasise too strongly what it meant to me to be able to listen to the advice of older Middlesex cricketers. The learning process never stops. Things do change from one generation to the next, I appreciate, but the basics do not, and I refuse to believe that even the most gifted modern player can never learn something he didn't know.

For well over a hundred years one generation has passed on its accumulated wisdom, knowledge and experience to the next. It has, more often than not, been appreciated, and has provided a beneficial and harmonious evolution in the game. It would be the ultimate tragedy if that came to an end.

Those are the thoughts of my friend P. H. Parfitt and I am happy to endorse them. They are exactly the sort of things Parf and I discuss on the occasions when we have had one of our family dinner parties. Our wives smile indulgently and leave us to get on with it, but I am sure that cricketers of our generation will understand exactly what we are getting at and why such conversations are valuable.

More than that, they are the stuff of memories and that, after all, is what this book is about. We all have our cricketing memories – players, officials, spectators – and they are precious to all of us. It has been my pleasure to share a few with cricket-lovers everywhere.

Index